# COWBOY

# POETRY

### and

## *Barn*
## *Sour*
## *Verse*

## By V. June Blevins Collins

# COWBOY POETRY

## AND

## BARN SOUR

## VERSE

By
V. June (Blevins) Collins

All rights reserved. No part of this publication shall be reproduced or transcribed in any form, except in brief quotation used in article reviews.

Edited By
**Wilhelmina Warick**
And
**Nadine Rogers**

2003
Published By
Collins Desktop

Printed in the United States by
Mosaic Press LLC
Happy Camp, CA.

ISBN # 0-9748755-0-3

LIBRARY OF CONGRESS
#
Pending

CONTENT

| Title | Pages |
|---|---|
| Appreciation and Acknowledgement | i |
| Dedication | ii |
| Introduction | iii |
| About Author | iv |
| Such Is My Life | A to Z+Za+Zb |
| Life's Poem Pages | Zc-Zd |
| Early Start | 1 |
| Monte Mom's Horse | 7 |
| Damper Smart | 9 |
| Pa and Charlie | 11 |
| Brand Registration 1915 of I. M. Blevins' | 12 |
| Brands in I. M. Blevins' 1890 brand book | 13 |
| Hayrack Chores (dedication) | 14 |
| Hayrack Chores | 15 |
| Branding (an explanation) | 16 |
| Branding Time | 17 |
| Long Shirt-tail | 21 |
| Evelyn, Sprout and June | 24 |
| Sprout | 25 |
| Jim | 27 |
| Coe with Mike when a foal | 30 |
| Mike (The Clydesdale) | 31 |
| Virginia Josephine | 33 |
| Old Fence | 36 |
| Fences | 37 |
| Pole Gate | 37 |
| Fence with wires dropped for winter | 40 |
| Fence Fixin' | 41 |
| Split Rail Corral | 44 |
| Tango, photo | 45 |
| Tango | 45 |
| Noon Hour Reprieve Painting | 49 |
| Noon Hour Reprieve | 50 |
| Distant Whispers | 53 |
| Wicked Wire Of The West | 55 |
| Locust Tree Post Raymond Place | 58 |
| Blue | 59 |
| Homeward Bound | 60 |
| Tracks photo | 62 |
| Tracks | 63 |
| Passion | 66 |
| Bronze Dansay (Dancer) | 67 |
| Sheep Rock | 71 |
| Sunset On Sheep Rock | 72 |
| Doc | 73 |
| Candy, Artise and Cappie | 75 |
| Candy and Natural Sweet | 76 |
| Jesse on Bogie | 79 |
| Ramrod Brewer.........1966 | 80 |
| Jess and Candy | 81 |

| | |
|---|---|
| Brewer family, and Dean, Candy and V. June | 82 |
| Cultivating He Goes | 83 |
| Call Of The Wind (Drawing) | 85 |
| Hungry Waters........1965 | 87 |
| Forks of Salmon Bridge after 1964 Flood | 90 |
| Jacket Retreat | 91 |
| Snow Comes Again In April...1967 | 92 |
| Springs Restless Sunshine | 93 |
| Beating The Heat..........1967 | 95 |
| My After Thoughts (1993) | 99 |
| Poetry's Assumed Names | 101 |
| Sulphur (The Buckskin Filly) | 102 |
| Blizzard Bier | 105 |
| On The Smoky "C"......1969 | 107 |
| Early And Late | 109 |
| Chow Time.................1970 (drawing) | 111 |
| Pollen Spring Pollen | 112 |
| Horse tracks on Mt Shasta | 113 |
| We Have Legends | 114 |
| Six Hard Spots Six Stones | 115 |
| Legend of Siskiyou (drawing) | 116 |
| Buckskin and Duns Dozing | 122 |
| Buckskin Acres (Splash -Remodel) | 123 |
| Cowboy In Cabbage Patch..1972 | 126 |
| Happy Buck-Appy..........1973 | 128 |
| Trail Class.............1975 | 133 |
| Pinks Day | 134 |
| Pink Photo | 137 |
| Harrington Lake Or Bust | 142 |
| Wistful Wildernes | 146 |
| Yellowstone Ride | 157 |
| Chief Joseph Trail Rides | 158 |
| Yellowstone Appy's | 159 |
| Severns' Dog, Ruff | 165 |
| June & Keith Severns Mexico Olymp1968-- | 168 |
| Friend Of Friends.......1975 | 169 |
| Bebe | 170 |
| Pinks Call..............1974 | 172 |
| Ochoco Rendezvous ( East of Prineville) | 176 |
| Friendships Endure 1930's - 2003 | 179 |
| Sonny Currie on Cooley and dog Hought | 180 |
| Camp Creek Boat Ramp, Wiley Cow Used | 181 |
| Currie.................1990 | 182 |
| Don's Runway Golf Cart | 185 |
| Cowboy | 187 |
| *Cowboy sculpture By Starritt* | 188 |
| Rock And Walk | 190 |
| Wheels To Deal | 191 |
| V. June and Three Wheeler | 192 |
| Kentucky Rides | 195 |
| Domino | 196 |
| Wont's Of Youth | 200 |
| Way It Is | 201 |
| Ol' Gin Bob | 202 |

| | |
|---|---|
| Sound Barrier | 207 |
| Old Pinch Bottom | 208 |
| Off Balance | 209 |
| Salmon River | 210 |
| Stan Cooley | 212 |
| Stan's Stone Boatin' Steer | 212 |
| Baling Wire | 215 |
| Baling Twine | 216 |
| Politition's Mistake | 218 |
| Second Childhood | 220 |
| Dreams | 222 |
| Runaway Truck Ramps on Siskiyou Mountain | 224 |
| Flight Of The Runaway Truck Ramp | 225 |
| Wills Wiles and Wont's | 228 |
| Parts And Pieces | 230 |
| To Elko For Another Year | 233 |
| Mileage Check | 234 |
| Packers, Brogans And Lacers | 235 |
| Other Boot Reasons | 238 |
| Night Before Christmas | 239 |
| After Christmas | 242 |
| What Age-(Watt-Age) | 243 |
| Tailholt, Mailboxes | 244 |
| Cow's Reputation | 246 |
| Velma and Rue' 25th | 248 |
| Barn Sour (Ol' Coots) | 250 |
| Klamath River Flood Scars | 252 |
| Cowboy Poetry, Hats Awake and Asleep | 253 |
| INDEX | 254 |
| Among My Pages | 257 |
| Nadine Rogers, Wilhelmina Warick, Editor | 260 |

# IN APPRECIATION
# AND
# ACKNOWLEDGMENT

To special friend, Bill Diehm, (now deceased) for encouragement and guidelines on my venturing toward and into the unknown world of my first book. I valued your opinion. To hear you say, "It must be published, I do thank you.

Thanks to my good friend, Nadine Rogers, with her sincere inspiration, encouragement and help where needed. A driving force in keeping my nose on the grind-stone, as a "must" project. Gratefully I accept her needed expertise and final review.

The author sincerely thanks good friend Wilhelmina Warick, for her volunteer, caring, and editing services in reviewing this manuscript and verifying its accuracy. Without your and Nadine's help, I would find myself dead in the water, mired in my "Puddle of Poetry," having a boat, rudder and sail, but no wind.

Special thanks goes to Gary Marlow, David Lee Rose, Karen Currie, Betty Cooley, Brice and Pat Martin and my husband, Jerry Collins, for use of their photos here in noted.

COVERS and ARTWORK - By: V. June Collins
CLIP ART pages #16-72-83-169-185-222-235-238-251 and back cover, used from Microsoft Publisher.

Interpretations or errors remaining, are author's sole responsibility.

*Those Monies received by The Genealogical Society of Siskiyou County, **from their sales of this book**, is a donation from V. June & Jerry Collins. **90% going to the Rose L. (Hicks) Brown Memorial Endowment Fund,** (a perpetual fund) where interest **only**, shall be used for the Society's livelihood, desires, plans, growth and or buildings. **10% shall go to the Genealogical Societies General Operating Expense Account**.*

V. June Collins

DEDICATION

It is with great pleasure I dedicate this
compilation to my husband, Jerry.

He has been a continual supportive force
in making its reality possible.

Photo by Gary Marlow

June and Jerry Collins

# INTRODUCTION

I have seen where other Cowboy Poets have remarked that if a city slicker does not quite understand their lingo, so be it! They say guidelines will not be added. However, I feel many urban dwellers still have the yearning for a rural way of life, and its every day happenings, with cravings for that bit of country that dwells in many of us.

Therefore, contrary to these rules, I have decided to add occasional explanations where I feel a better understanding might be gained by the reader, whether urban or rural, black or white, or amber. It is my desire for my reader to gladly be lead among my pages, accompanied by the feel of a friendly handshake. To indulge themselves while enjoying the happenings, and experiences, like a personal echo.

Most of my verses are keyed from true happenings, while others are from demanding thoughts, and feelings. Some are foolishness in the home corral, or when my mind takes a holiday.

The poems in my book are written in much the same tone as I speak. My sayings are my family's words passed down through generations and then stamped, and ingrained, to become a part of me. I was surrounded by ranch life, and steeped in this atmosphere for years living, and growing up in a rural community on a Central Oregon cattle ranch and ranger station.

SUCH IS MY LIFE - has been included, among my pages. I feel my life belongs among my writings, that you, the reader, may enjoy an opportunity to acquaint yourselves with me, through my background, and understand my writing a bit better.

The old adage that says, "You can take the girl from the ranch, but you can't take the ranch out of the girl," truly applies. Like a brand, if it takes, it lasts a life time.

V. June (Blevins) Collins

# About The Author

Photo By Sandy Crebbins, Shasta Studio

# V. June Blevins Collins

BORN
AND
RAISED
IN
THE
OCHOCO'S
NURTURED
IN
THE
SISKIYOU'S

Photographer Unknown

Awilda Josephine (O'Kelley) Blevins, and daughters, Evelyn Irene 3 1/2 year, and V. June, 6 weeks old.

Photos By Isaac Blevins

Family fishing on Marks Creek. Coe J. Blevins, (grandmother); Lee E. Blevins, (Dad) with fishing pole; Awilda Josephine Blevins, mother; Evelyn I. Blevins (sister 5 years); V. June Blevins (2years).

Awilda Josephine Blevins;
Evelyn Blevins, (5 years);
V. June Blevins, (2years)
At ranch house front gate.

V. June Blevins,

(2 years old) Sitting against the front gate at her grandparents ranch, with her lap full of cats.

Grandmother, Coe's, black dog called Pink, is baby sitting the outfit.

Photo By Ike Blevins

June in the orchard at Upper McRae place, where grandparents, Ike and Coe Blevins, moved each summer. June is proudly showing off her new catch of the day, a trapped Sage-Rat.

Ike was foreman of Farquer McRae ranches for many years, as well as running their own ranch, 20 miles east of Prineville, Oregon on the Upper Ochoco.

Photo By Ike Blevins

Photo By Brainerd Studios

V. June Blevins (17 years) Graduate of Grants Pass, Oregon High School, 1934

Photo by Ray Macfarlane.

1942 G. J."Jerry" Collins; Michael Lee Collins; V. June (Blevins) Collins, holding, 6 mo old Lael Gareld Collins. Standing beside our 1936 Chevy.

Photo By Jack Young Camera Shop, Yreka California

V. June Collins 1960

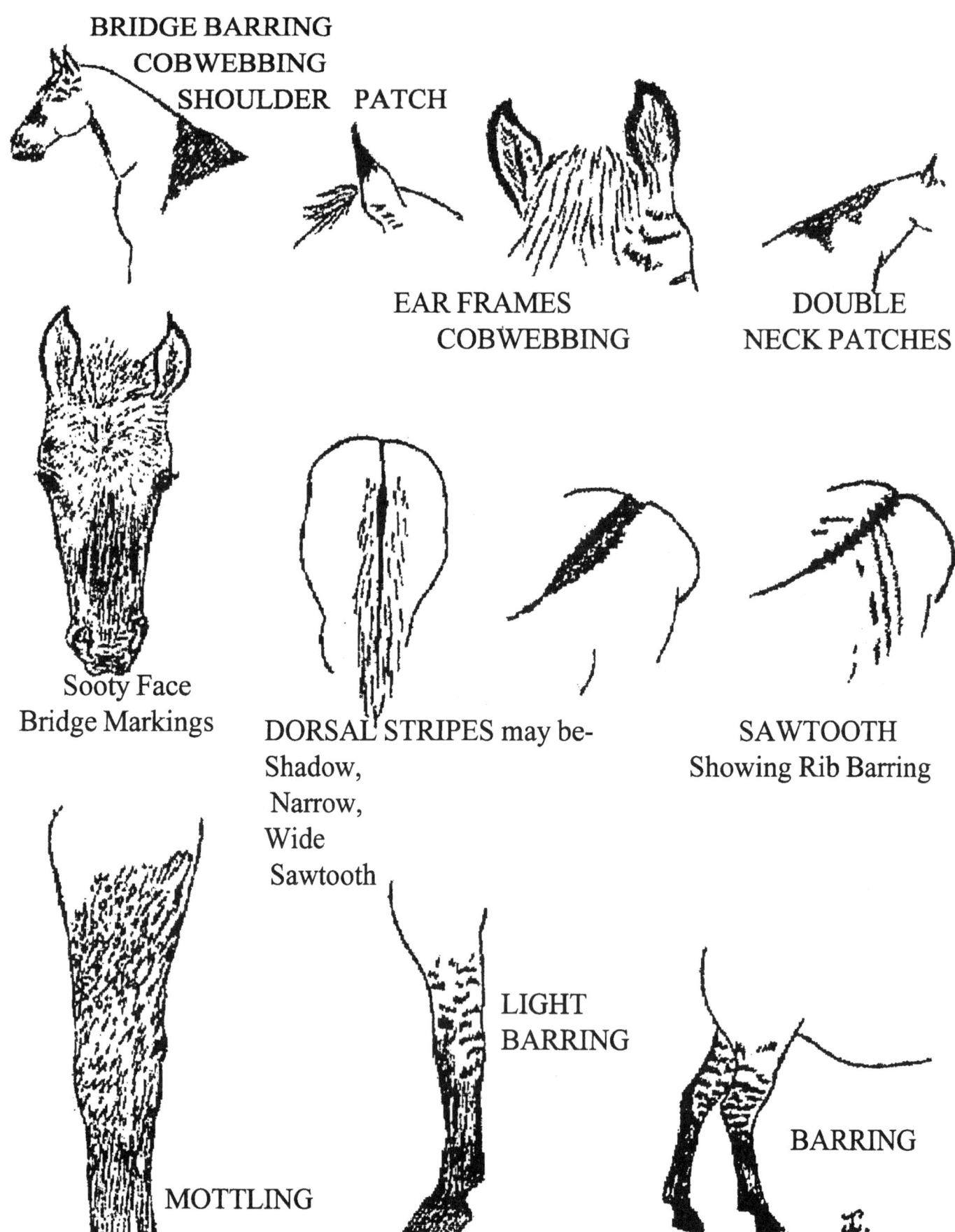

Markings shown, are those used for many years by The American Buckskin Registry Association in their "Rules and Information Booklet" which were drawn By V. June Collins for their use.

## MEANING OF ABRA INSIGNIA

The breed of Buckskin, Grulla, Dun and Red Dun, takes its deserving place in horsedom, wearing its crown in regal pride. Shown in a hard luck horseshoe, denoting struggle for survival, this breed has endured through neglect and abuse. Yet it regularly produces its own color, the original color of nearly every known breed of today. Held together by strength, a golden chain "B-U-C-K-S-K-I-N" of nine links, alloyed together with "G-R-U-L-L-A and D-U-N-" to restore, nurture, treasure and become ever stronger.

The banner of the "American Buckskin" rightfully continues to fly.

V. June Collins designed this Insignia, and in 1967 it was accepted as the logo, of The American Buckskin Registry Association in Redding, California, with their permission to encompass the original horses head into the design, which the Registry used during its early beginning years.

A FEW
HIGH NOON
RESTS
AMONG
THE
15 YEARS
OF
APPALOOSA
CHIEF JOSEPH
100 MILE
TRAIL RIDES

Photo By Gary Marlow

1976, V. June along the trail on a lunch break, of the Appaloosa Chief Joseph 100 mile trail ride.

Photo by Jerry Collins

1979, Lunch break on a high plateau above the Salmon River, in Idaho. Rest is where you can catch it.

Photo By Jim Evans

June, on Blue, and Jerry on Misty, high in the Bitteroot Mountains of Montana. 1985 segment of Chief Joseph Trail Ride.

Photo By Jerry Collins

V. June Collins catching a bit of rest after lunch, atop a high mountain between Spencer, Idaho, and West Yellowstone. During another segment of Appaloosa, Chief Joseph Trail Ride.

Photo By Gary Marlow

1986 awards night recognition along National,"Nee Mee Poo," (the peoples) Trail, on the Chief Joseph Trail Ride.  June received a plaque for being the first person to finish the full, 1300 miles distance, on the same rented horse, "Blue," owned by the Bill Schulz family of Wayan, Idaho.  (Nearly needless to say, after 15 years of riding Blue, I had the same feeling toward him, as if he had been my very own horse.)

Photo By V. June Collins

"Blue"

  For fifteen years Blue was my transportation each year, for another hundred miles on the trails of another Chief Joseph Ride. He soon became a very special addition to my life.
You may think only dogs sniff to make or renew acquaintances. Not so! Blue would sniff the bottom of my trousers cuffs, and feet, each time another ride made its renewed appearance. As if to say, Oh! You again! Just checking. With what appeared to be satisfaction, he would then return to his usual interest of eating.

  I have staked him a number of nights to sage brush, in front of our tent on a necessary very short tie of about ten inches, so he could not easily get a foot over his tie rope. All without a hassle. Only his breaking daylight, soft whinney, let me know it was time to awake from my nights slumber. Like clockwork, his reminder was saying, "It's time for my chow."

  Our communion grew, and was felt between us. Trust and respect gathered strength along our path like a friendship. His memory has left me this treasure.

Photo by Sandy Crebbins, Camera Shasta

V. June Collins - Picture taken for use in the local, "Cowboy Poetry Festival Program," a fund raising, fun project, held annually at the Community Theater in Yreka, California. It has been received by many, from its beginning, with great acceptance as a much looked forward to, pleasure. April or December performances have continued for the past eleven years, as of 2003.

# SUCH IS MY LIFE

V. June (Blevins) Collins was born in Prineville, Oregon, daughter of Lee Edward Blevins and Awilda Josephine, (O'Kelley) Blevins. Raised on the Ochoco, 20 and 27 miles east of Prineville, Oregon.

My sister, Evelyn, and I spent much of our early lives with our Grandparents, Isaac M."Ike" Blevins and Cora J. (Miller) Blevins. We stayed with them during school term, when the weather got extremely cold. They lived closer to our school, and we spent a lot of time with them during summer, too. We helped with needed chores at hand, learning while feeding, milking, working cattle, and sheep, both horseback and on the ground. In spring, we helped fix drift fences, brand cattle and drive them to the summer range on Lookout Mountain. We rode range, checked cattle, and hauled 25 pound salt sacks on pack horses to fill salt troughs. These were often made from hollowed out logs. Today, salt blocks are used instead of loose salt. Come fall, we gathered and pushed cattle from the high country to lower elevations. Then came a week or so of all day rides, gathering stragglers and pushing them back down trails toward the ranch, before winter weather.

Evelyn, and I rode seven miles to school on horseback, from Ochoco Ranger Station both morning and evening, except, when tempertures brought tears to our eyes, forcing us to get off and walk to stay warm. A well remembered highlight of evening rides homeward, are races up the road to see who, after a quick stop, could bail off, tie her horse to the front fence, and arrive first, at the front door of our Grandparents house for a special snack, usually a slab of pie which Grandmother, *Coe, baked nearly every day. Just the necessary fuel needed, we felt, to get us on up the road the next 5 miles.

My first real job came during summer's haying season. I, being low man on the totem pole, started out as others before me had, driving derrick. I had turned seven years old that past May, and was chaffing at the bit, to do what I thought was something more important.

*I called my grandmother Coe.

This job entailed hooking a hook, onto a single tree, that dragged on the ground behind our old gentle work mare, Nellie, which was attached to a cable running back through the barn. Upon hearing the call, "Take her away," I would lead her out from the barn, pulling the cable with Nellie straining under the load, behind her, until I heard a call from one of the stackers yell, "Trip her!" Only then, as the load was released, could I unhook the cable attached to the single tree. I would unhook and lead her in a wide ark or half circle (needing to get her turned around, without letting her step into the chains dragging along behind her.), Then I would proceed to lead her back along the same path to the barn, where I would make another wide half-circle to get her turned around facing away from the barn and hook the cable back up to the single tree again, ready to travel the same well beaten path, waiting to hear the net setter, again holler, "Take her away!"

This hook attached to the cable lead back through the barn and through some pulleys, up into the cone of the barn roof. There it was attached to the carriage, which ran on a track back and forth from the front to the back of barn. At the far end, or front of the barn, the hook, attached to the far end of cable would be attached to the net, outstretched on the ground, laying in wait for a fill. It was filled with hay, from Buckrake drivers and, teams waiting and ready to deliver another load in place, then hoisted up into barn. Each time Nellie was lead out away from barn, she pulled another load of hay up to the carriage which it latched onto to be carried along the track the full length of the barn, or to where by choice, it was deposited in hay *mow, where next, the stackers decided it was most needed.

Hay was placed in large single loads on the net, by a person driving a teams of horses, hitched to the Buck Rake. The team pushed the Buck-Rake's long, wooden pole teeth, (of about 12 feet long), ahead of them. They gathered up smaller shocks of hay in the field into a single, extra large load and placed these loads on top of stretched out net. The Buck-Rake driver, would then lower the teeth of the Buck Rake. This placed the weight of the hay onto net. With ease, the teeth could then be backed off and out smoothly, from under the hay load and away from the net. The Buck-Rake driver would then be on his way, for another load. The Net Tender gathered together both of the pole sides of the net, and attached the hook from the far end of the cable, and yelled loud enough for me to hear, "Take 'er away".

*hay mow: The space inside barn where hay is stored.

I soon learned to listen more closely, for sounds of different voices, mingled in among other voice's directions and conversations. A familiar holler "My signal" to lead Nellie out from the barn, again, on the well worn path, to pull another load up into the barn, or haystack, which ever it might be. The hay stackers, would soon yell, "Tripper!" and I'd see the load release, as Nellie relaxed.

The Net man simutaneously dragged the unhooked cable back through the barn to his hook up place, as he pulled back on the net, with an attached rope. He then reset it, for another load.

This routine, had a way of getting old, pretty fast, even for an enthusiastic, new beginner. But, I also knew full well, that I didn't dare quit, for a promotion might be in sight. So this remained my job for a number of years.

When I reach the age of nine, it was felt I was old and strong enough to drive the team on the dump rake, which was a much looked forward to advancement, I might say. Soon I was raking all the fields. It also made running derrick just another job that had to be done.

Yet, I was looking forward to that, which was a little bit out of reach. I still had my sights set on running the Buck-Rake. I turned thirteen by the time this finally happened and achieved this looked forward to honor. However, my Buck-Rake job lasted only one year. It seems, Buck Rakes had become obsolete.

Because of the ill health of my Grandfather, one winter my sister and I would be up before daylight each morning, harness and hitch up the team to the wagon, and drive across the creek, to the far side of the field, to the hay stack and loaded the hay-rack with hay. Then we took turns driving in a large circle while the other one scattered the load by the fork full to the hungry bawling cattle. We returned to the barn, unharnessed, watered and fed the team. By necessity, we quickly changed clothes and headed out for Howard School, District #5, an all-grade elementary school we attended, about a half mile distance from our Grandparents ranch house.

I attended this school from the first through my seventh grade. Eighth grade year was at the only elementary school in the town of Prineville, Oregon. Sister, Evelyn, had started high school, and mother rented the Reams house in town, for the school term, where we spent each week and drove back home on weekends.

My Grandmother (Coe), passed away in the fall, of September 1930. Whenever we went back to the ranch it felt different and lonely. I missed her hearty, jovial laugh, and enthusiastic personality. Gone was the glow and chatter, an important part of life was so missing, and had gone out of our life there. I felt restless, unsettled, almost uneasy. My grandmother Coe, was a great and independent lady. Her leaving left a deep empty space, which touched my life in large portions. Non-replaceable. But, we were blessed to have been left with many precious memories, strung like beads to enjoy and savor, these many years.

The next spring I turned fourteen. That summer I was asked by my grandfather to take on the job of cooking for the haying crew, all by myself. Grandmother was gone. My mom said, "You can do it!" I was satisfied that I could cook plain food, so the task was accomplished without knowing enough to be apprehensive or scared. The crew survived, too.

About a year later, in 1931, my Granddad "Pa," Isaac Blevins, died of a heart attack. I felt dropped into another world. I had spent much time with him. I needed his strong presence. I had not told him. I just didn't know how much I'd miss him, until he was gone. I never did see "Pa" get mad. My mother said, "In my life time, I only saw him mad once."

My legacy from Pa, which he instilled in me, was while working with animals, the prime importance of controlling my temper (which I had plenty of), for when temper is lost, so quickly, are the advantages of teaching. Gains become slow or become nonexistent. I had watched him during trying circumstances, he was an example. Though it was difficult for me to remember, in the beginning, to call a halt to a problem and cool off, or even until another day. It is far more difficult to undo something that would have been avoided had temper not raised its ugly head.

Note: My father was called "Papa" by Evelyn and I, and by the time my two younger sisters (Virginia Lee and Olive Ruth Loraine) came along, seven and ten years later, they called him "Dad." He answered to both.

Only, a short time after Pa's death, Papa received notice of a transfer from Ochoco National Forest into Siskiyou National Forest, to be headquartered at Grants Pass, Oregon, into law enforcement undercover work, as a Forest Service Detective and Finger Print Expert. He accepted the challenge.

People were then setting fires for work, and hiring on to help put the fires out, as well as stealing and stashing supplies off of pack-strings, that were going to fires loaded with supplies for the fire fighters. This practice had gotten out of hand while forests were being ravaged severely. Papa was sent in, with firm intentions of stopping this practice, which in due time he did. A ring leader and a goodly number of fire setters were apprehended and sent to prison. This practice of setting incendiary fires, became very unpopular to be involved in.

However, in preparation for this transfer, many decisions had to be made. The home ranch was sold. *These were depression times.* All our regular horses on the place, were sold for $2.50 a head, except for my sister's chestnut horse, "Peanuts," which brought $15.00. I knew my mare would also have to be sold. I could not bare the thought. I cried and begged. Papa said, "No! Only one horse, could go with us."

In those days we had never trailered our horses, we rode to where we wanted to go. Other people's horses were trucked on occasion. I didn't even know anyone that used a trailer. Apparently Papa did, and with ingenuity built an open air trailer, for the purpose of bringing one horse with us, on our move.

The horse Papa intended to bring along was his bay saddle horse "Big," which was an excellent walker, of five miles an hour. However, "Big" was soon thoroughly convinced my dad was trying to kill him, and would have no part of his rolling affair. Though, not before he had become bruised skinned, and thoroughly disillusioned with the human race.

This all took place in a short period of time before we were scheduled to leave and left little time to gentle or feed him into accepting this contraption, with any idea of climbing aboard, without still insisting on jumping immediately, right back out.

"Big," was, by common sense, eliminated as not desirable for this long haul, because of the short period of time Papa had to work with him before leaving. Papa knew he would be loading and unloading along the way. He came into the kitchen one evening where I was and said, "June, "we are going to take your mare instead of "Big."

I could hardly believe my ears. Wow! I was delighted! I jumped and danced in excitement. It had turned out for sure, my mare and I were the lucky ones. She had been given to me when I was ten years of age, by my grandparents, Pa and Coe, and I had named her "Jungles." She was the only horse on the place that would load into Papa's horse trailer with acceptance. So now, she would not be sold with the rest of the horses. I was elated! All because she'd do most anything I asked her to do. She had faith in me not asking of her the impossible. Now she could travel to our new abode with us. Papa would use her in his work, whenever necessary.

Consequently, Papa sold "Big" for $35.00 to a man by the name of Grissom who had been wanting to buy him for some time, because of his ability to walk so much faster than average horses. Both Evelyn's and my mare would walk a few steps and continually need to throw in three or four jig steps in order to keep up.

We left Ochoco Station at 5:00 AM on a cold, dark morning in 1932 with "Jungles" dangling along behind, in the trailer. In those days the roads were gravel at best, and slow going. On reaching higher elevation between Bend and Klamath Falls, the rain turned to snow, and got heavier. Jungle's face was soon plastered white, like a mask. Finally my dad stopped the car and asked us to **fork** out one of the wool army blankets from the back seat. My mother supplied a number of large safety pins, and he wrapped and pinned the blanket onto Jungles' shivering chest and withers, to ease some of her discomfort. We drove on, through the snow. It gradually turned to sleet and finely back to steady, cold rain. We girls had cried our eyes dry, in sad lonely thoughts-- feeling both sorry for ourselves, as well as for Jungles. Much anxiety was felt, for the plight we'd found ourselves in. It seemed like the end of the world, having left behind all our friends of our young lives that we knew.

By the time we arrived on the other side of Klamath Falls, Oregon, where we were to leave "Jungles for the night at a ranch house, it was dark. It had taken us all day to cover the distance, that today we cover in less than five hours. Papa then drove back to Klamath Falls to the Winema Hotel where he had made reservations. There we spent the night.

The next day dawned, March 17, 1932, "Saint Patrick's Day". Our road led us over the mountain, via Green Springs Highway. Through Keno, Ashland, and through Medford. In the afternoon we arrived in Grants Pass, Oregon, where Papa had rented a house for us, on North 2nd Street.

In a few days the big truck arrived with all the rest of our trappings. The house began to take on a distant feel of home, yet rain continued for three solid weeks. We were from a far drier climate, and felt much like disgruntled, misplaced rats, as we hunkered close by the fire, trying to keep warm. From our bedroom window each night, we watched the lonely beacon on Tokay rotate around and around, lashing its probing rays through and across the valley's dense fog that settled in, and hung like a shroud over this damp, lonely, unfriendly feeling place.

Oak wood, we had never used before. When it is green, it is nearly impossible to keep a fire going, let alone a warm one. Somehow my mother made the last ditch effort, necessary to accomplish this, and all the time trying to cheer us up with small talk.

Yes, finally the sun came out and we did make new friends. The Rogue River became our wide, new swimming hole, that couldn't stand still. It soon became a regular occurance, during summer, that in order to go swimming, we gladly ankled it along on our shanks pony's a mile each way nearly every day. I became a good swimmer as my skin turned a copper tan of a dusky, smokey hue. Yes, while here at this house, away from home, my old memories soon became easier to deal with and rememberings got farther apart. I began to like Grants Pass - all except the ever present hovering of fog and rain during the winter months.

After this move, I finishing my sophomore year, and graduated from the Grants Pass, Oregon, high school in 1934. However, I then found a need to sell my mare, "Jungles" in order to further my education. My difficult choice. I Received the sum of $45.00 for her, and never thereafter saw her again. Through time, I still found myself looking for her among all the strange groups of horses. Thoughts of her have been many, for my gentle, and kind friend. (Life often deals a strange bedfellow to live with.)

I went on to Pacific Beauty College in Portland, Oregon in the fall. I received a Cosmetology degree the following year, with a gold seal on my diploma signifying a grade above 95. I worked in that field of work, for a time.

The money I received when I sold my mare (may sound measly today), but then it was important. I could, and did, rent a tiny apartment with a single bed. It had a hot plate, a row of shelves, and a chest of drawers, with a share in a community bath room, all on the third floor of a walk up apartment building, for $5.00 a month. Hamburger then was ten cents a pound. I would buy half a pound. I had no refrigeration, so I needed to eat that before it would spoil. Coffee was twenty five cent a pound. The heat I had came from the tenants below me, who could afford heat. It seaped upward. I don't ever remember being especially cold there.

Later on, another girl from school, who was from Klamath Falls, and I rented a bigger room for $10.00 a month. We shared a double bed. It was on the ground floor and closer to school. It had a two burner gas hot plate, plus a wood heating stove in the corner, but we didn't have money to buy wood for it. It was pretty brisk on winter mornings. We would quickly hop out of bed, get dressed, and put on our coats. Then we would get our breakfast of oatmeal, with four chopped-up dates in it. We would buy one pound of dates each week, and by dividing them, it gave us four each morning for breakfast. Oh yes, we also saved all paper and bags accumulated during the week. On Sunday morning we would light a fire in the stove after breakfast, and joyfully absorb its friendly warmth, sitting a while enjoying a hot cup of coffee.

I married, in 1935, had a son, Michael Lee in 1937, divorced in 1939, and also worked as retail clerk at the then new Montgomery & Wards store in Grants Pass, Oregon.

In 1940 I married Gareld J. "Jerry" Collins, in Reno, Nevada. Jerry was then employed at Littrell Parts in Yreka, California, as a shipping clerk, at $100.00 a month. As newlyweds, we rented a small house on Blake Street, at $20.00 a month, which Jerry had helped finish, for our rental, from Tommy and Anna Cordoza. In a short time Jerry was advanced to counterman, and on to an outside salesman.

Jerry was transferred to Dunsmuir in 1941. We, Jerry, Michael and I moved. We stayed three weeks with Ermine "Battie" and Hattie Batson. Meanwhile, we bought a small piece of ground in Champion Park, in south Dunsmuir. Then we drove to Sacramento and bought a Sheridan trailer house to live in, because we felt we needed to start accumulating equity in a house instead of paying rent. It had a front and back door, something new then. Our spirits were high. Of course it was not self contained-- none were at that time, so buying a chemical toilet was the next necessity. Jerry hurriedly dug a septic tank and planted a light pole for electricity on our new property. We moved in and were pleased with all of our accomplishments.

We were looked at by some, at that time, as being nomads-- someone not quite to be trusted. If you lived in a house with wheels, you might just drive away in the middle of the night. Some of our friends distanced themselves from us. We tried to consider the sources, and not to let this bother us much. We had confidence that we were doing the best thing for us, and were happy with our decision.

We soon put in a garden and enjoyed our fresh vegetables. Jerry added a small room in his spare time, where we then had our washtrays and washing machine, and finally a refrigerator to replace the icebox. That refrigerator is still being used today (2003), in our recreation room of our home and it is quieter than the new variety, up stairs. I might add, about the same time as our trailer adventure, Jerry's sister and husband, also bought a trailer in Medford, Oregon. We went to help them find a place to park it. They too, could find not one Auto Court that would rent to them, saying, that their regular tenants might not stay, if they rented to someone on wheels. They finely leased a strip of ground from a friend. Little did we know then that we were pioneers of the R.V. Evalution. "Homes On Wheels", which today, are bulging out and into, all over-night facilities, and beaconing more in, as well.

One cool, sunny day December 7, 1941, Jerry and I were out cleaning off old vines and stalks from our past summers garden, which we had neglected to get done earlier. Battie Batson drove down from his house to give us some shocking words; Pearl Harbor was being bombed by the Japanese. We were numb struck! Anxious, stirred, angry and degraded, even uneasy, all at the same time. It was hard to comprehend. We dropped everything and went inside and turned on the radio to listen. What we heard was confusion, devastation and destruction being described from those under attack. War was declared. Many young men joined the armed forces, others were drafted. The home front lived in an uneasy state, not knowing what was coming next.

Our son, Lael Gareld Collins, was born June 26, 1942, in the early part of WW II years. Jerry was transferred back to Yreka, four month later. It was decided to close down the Dunsmuir store and move merchandise from there to Yreka, because of man shortage, and the need to operate with less personnel. Many items and things were then frozen, or on ration until the war was over, and must be allotted only to those eligible, however, long that would be.

We moved back to Yreka in October of 1942, and rented a small house from Mark Sylva and his wife, across the street, from where Hall's car wash is today. We spent much of the winter there. Those large poplar trees along Poor George's Restaurant at that time graced Sylva's little Ranchette, including the duck pond and much greenery. The Mark Sylvas', are parents of Dick Sylva, who today prominently figures in the establishment of the old trails in Siskiyou County and elsewhere.

Then the house on Blake Street, that we had lived in when we were first married, became vacant. We moved back into it. Parking our trailer house along side it, for the rest of winter.

In the spring of 1945, we sold our trailer, for $900.00. With that, and some borrowed money, we bought into Littrell Parts, and became partners with Al Littrell, as did Battie Batson.

In 1946, we bought our first house, North of Yreka, for $6,000.00 from Jack and Rosalee Brazil. We lived there until February 1947, when again we were transferred back to Dunsmuir.

We sold this home, and rented a house in Dunsmuir to live in across the highway, from the ball park. After a time, I started playing softball with a team organized with Al Marske and Ray Arnold as coaches. We played under the name of "Dunsmuir Hornets." In jeans and bright yellow, terry sweatshirts, which had a big angry hornet stenciled on backs, designed by Concha Baca. Our first sponsor was Bob's Dairy. Later on we were sponsored by Corral Resort, and were then decked out in royal blue uniforms. We played, Yreka, Weed, and Redding on scheduled nights with much determination, winning more than our share of games. We also were the first organization to donate moneys toward the night lights, for the Dunsmuir ball park. Our team pitcher, Alicia Baca, later joined the Navy and played professional ball making quite a name for herself, as did her sister, Concha Baca, our third baseman, did similarly in the Marines.

In the fall of 1948 while still living in Dunsmuir, we were able to buy another special horse, my Buckskin mare, "Tango." We, since that time, have had horses, and have kept busy working, riding, training and showing as many as fifteen, for nearly thirty years.

By 1950, the freeway was coming to town and it forced us to move from the house near the ball park, because they needed our ground space. We then bought the old Weaver place on Florence Avenue. I continued to play ball. The San Mateo girls team from the Bay area, played against us a number of times, on their way through to Canada on vacations. They also played other teams along the way. We girls also went down to San Mateo, and returned the favor. Our uniforms had changed color to green. We were called the Merchanett's when the local Merchant became our sponsors.

In 1955, we again came back to Yreka to the main store, where it was decided Jerry needed to be. Since that time we have made Yreka our home, accomplishing the 63 year mark, of living in Siskiyou County. For many years I typed up forms, made stencils and ran copies from the Gestetner machines, for all inner office paper forms needed within the stores.

The first Buckskin horse show in the nation was held at the Golden Fair Grounds, Yreka, California in 1965. We received a first place award on our 1965 filly, "Sulpher Sannrush,"#P-400. I was actively involved, and have supplied foot work, in many capacities, towards the Annual Buckskin Horse Shows held in Yreka and Redding, each year thereafter, including the 1980 show. The fifth and last foal of her line, which we bred, raised, and registered in ABRA, was Three Grande Sannfela # P-3000 1975.

In 1967 I designed the insignia and Logo, for the American Buckskin Registry Association, Inc. It was voted on by the board and accepted, and is used internationally by ABRA. They now are in their 40th year of existence, (1963-2003.)

In 1970, I also started doing extra work, for some ten years, for the American Buckskin Registry Association (ABRA), in all capacities needed, without remuneration's, including hand and air brush painting of manes, tails, barring and dorsal stripes on trophies supplied by ABRA for their horse shows, that were sent out over the U. S. and Canadian Horseshows. I wrote a Dun and Buckskin research pamphlet used for identification purposes for ABRA. For many years, in their information pamphlet, my drawings and markings were used as descriptive examples for registration. I became a member in 1963, and am a life-time member. The first horse I registered was my mare, "Tango" Mala #P-98, in 1964. .

I have been involved with working and training horses most of my life, ours and those to be sold. When one has been kissed with the love of ranch life, and horses at an early age and it takes, it is like a special gold medallion, one wears within, for the rest of their life. I feel I have been blessed and among the privileged.

My husband, Jerry and I have ridden 15 segments on the Appaloosa

Chief Joseph 100 Mile Trail Rides. From Wallowa, Oregon, into and across Idaho, into Montana, through the Yellowstone, over the Absoroka Mountains of Wyoming, and back north to Bear Paw Montana, within 30 miles of the Canadian border. We also rode two more overlaps, of the CJTR. One of those was through Yellowstone Park, twice, seeing country that could not have been seen otherwise, but from the back of a horse.

I was awarded a plaque in 1984, for being the first person to have finished those 13 hundred miles of the CJTR, on same rented horse "Blue." Blue was owned by the Bill Shulz family of Wayan, Idaho. Blue soon was to feel like my own. After that *many wet blankets, an attachment arrives. We each learned and understood a great deal more about each others personalities, in the process. He is truly endeared in my memories, after riding him those many miles, into and out of, some unexpected happenings.

We have also ridden five hundred miles on the Sheltowee Ride (an Indian name given to Daniel Boone, meaning big turtle), in Kentucky, and Tennessee, plus two hundred miles on Apache Ride near the Mexico border, in Arizona, where again, our eyes have been filled with scenery, from the back of a horse. If hiking, one need to look where their feet are being planted, as well as lacking extra elevation which the horse provides. We both (Jerry, and I), rode rented horses on these rides, too, thereby being able to finish off at the end of the ride and do other things besides trailering horses home. We could then take another week at our leisure.

Hunting we have done a great deal of, and in earnest as seasons rolled around. Through our early years, we had much interest in filling our larder with food toward each coming winter. We did a great deal of fishing, in streams and lakes, some in the ocean. We both have killed quite a number of Buck deer, pheasants, ducks, geese and cotton tails. Jerry has killed a few bear also, which our family ate with relish. Coyotes, skunks and lots of digger squirrels tend to keep our eye sharp.

My hobbies, and interests other than horses are numerous. Writing and

---

***Wet blankets:** Every time you ride a horse, his sweat supplies a wet blanket undeneath the saddle, which you later remove after work. It takes lots of these sessions or wet blankets to know, and fully understand, as you train a horse.

poetry fills a special need as the urge often nudges. I have written somewhere in the vacinity of 400 poems, that I have copies of-- Some horsey, some otherwise. These stories of happenings close to home, I class as Barn Sour Verse, and stay at home variety. The list goes on.

I am interested in Photography and take lots of pictures. I have been the photographer on some of the rides we have participated in as well.

I took many night art classes from Jan Cozzolio in the 50's and 60's. drawing in pencil, ink, chalks, charcoal, pastel and Conte, and also painting in oils, watercolor, tempera, moe, plus color theory. Jan is a great teacher. I feel fortunate to have had this opportunity. Many a night I would be so excited about a subject she had presented, that I would start in again, upon getting home, and find daylight had arrived before I was ready to call it a day. I have also taken classes from a few others that did not have that ability to inspire students.

We were avid Rockhounds for many years, too. Hunting rocks and packing loads home in pack sacks on our backs. I also cut and polished them. For a number of years, we belonged to the Yreka Rock and Mineral Club from its beginning. A number of designs were presented for review, and the club voted for my design as their Logo. I was president and secretary for a number of terms. I did a great deal of Lapidary work, cutting, grinding, sanding and polishing a variety of semi precious stones into cabachons and jewlery, plus bigger slabs of jade, jasper, agate and petrified wood. I took many Geology classes during the 50's, and 60's, and acquired quite a number of College units in Geology.

I have been doing sewing, since an early age, and made many of our cloths during our earlier years, and still occasionally whip up something. Mending keeps the sewing machine from getting neglected, in today's busy schedule.

Meanwhile, through the years, we bought into, and owned Littrell Auto Parts Stores of California. Jerry established eleven Littrell Welding Supply Stores in California, Oregon and Nevada. We sold the Littrell Auto Parts stores to our son, Lael, and his wife Carolyn of Montague, California. They, for some time, have been sole owners of Littrell Parts Automotive Stores, in Yreka, Mt. Shasta, Susanville and M & M Auto Parts in Corning, California.

In 1988 we sold the eleven, Littrell Welding Supply Stores and Home Health Store to Airgas, of Radnor, Pennslyvania.

Son, Michael Lee Collins earlier retired from Collins Enterprises, Inc. (deceased) Feb 14, 1994,

I have made compilations of more than forty, three inch binders, of Genealogy on both my husband and my side of the family house. In the winter of 1999 I started compiling them into a computer, on "Family Tree Maker." to date some 3700 ancestors and descendents have been corraled and there's more information yet to pull out of binders.

Computer work also consists of my Autobiography, with many stories still hand written and not yet in the computer, some are still in the making. I have done a great deal of Biography work, on my mother to add to her poetry for the family--history of interest, stories of family goings on, etc. Life truly has been good to me, to have allowed me to taste and savor these special qualities in living.

For the past 39 years we have lived outside the town of Yreka, California, Siskiyou County, on a 40 acre place. Its first address was Rt. 1 Box 100A; then it became Rt. 1 Box 504. This also, became obsolete and the P. O. frowned on their use. Without moving we have attained still another number and address. I guess that's what they call progress.

I retired in 1989 from raising, showing and training Buckskin horses. Now only feeding pensioners: One Buckskin old mare, a Buckskin Appaloosa mare and a burro. My special Red Dun, saddle mare, Pink, left us in April 7, 2002 at the ripe old age of 35 years. In human years, that's equivalent to 105. Aged Dun mare, Shore, also deceased the same year.

Many years ago, thinking when my children were raised and no longer at home. I would have time to burn and could do many things I had planned.

This didn't happen that easy. Somewhere along line, I took on more obligations, while time marched on. Upon retiring, this same mentality surfaced again. Only by many extra hours of determination (above and beyond), can I get to my writing. I keep finding it waiting in the back seat, where it seems, to ends up.

All for the lack of time!
        I find, though its difficult
                I need to make time.
                        To put my arm around it, often,
                                    to nurture, and stay acquainted.

By V. June (Blevins) Collins

# LIFE'S POEM PAGES

## By V. June Collins

Started rounding up my verses,
Some were fat, while others lean.
As gathering them together,
Found others were in between.

Decided to put them on pages wide,
With print right down the middle.
Even verses fat or skinny like,
Would fit most like a fiddle.

For as my memory spoke to me,
In choosing each little docket.
Remembered kids reading funny books,
Then folded 'em up into their pocket.

My jeans also had tell tale lines,
That showed a books narrow size.
Much like guys, snuff can pockets,
Can't lie, from its disguise.

For I had one book of poems
Pages yellowed, and rather old.
That I had no need to roll up,
To push and shove or fold.

Was built to fit my hip pocket,
One I enjoyed on leisure times.
Those treasures among the pages,
Held joy, with special rhymes.

Then was made in size, just right,
For was known long years ago.
Must grab, time, for these readings,
Somewhere in between and on the go.

Now I guess have gone the distance
Back and forth and up and down.
For I'm still just a country gal,
That lives on the edge of town.

More than 400 poems accumulated,
Make many choices on my plate.
Some bound too taste better than others
Even in among the old, or up to date.

We will probably break a few rules,
From its size or by some convention.
But for a book to fit into hip pocket
Today, would attract but small attention.

I've found the need for a bit larger print.
Chances are, other eyes too, growing dim.
While some might read without their glasses
None, to be crowded off, the reading limb.

If these theories should fit your likings,
And you wish to travel, this same road.
Where I've made some dust, while writing,
'Cause, sometimes packing quite a load.

Relax a while and reminisce with me.
Just take some time to unwind.
Might be allowed to enjoy yourself,
Among my verses, stretch your mind.

Whichever path, you're traveling on,
Similar patterns or different modes.
Wishes you, to partake of communion,
Off down common kinds of roads.

I'll share with you my understanding,
Some feelings felt, most near to kin.
Down familiar, friendly, same roads.
Into places, often times, have been.

***AS TOLD MANY TIMES BY MY MOTHER:*** *Awilda Josephine (O'Kelley) Blevins: Papa was Fire Guard at Antler Station on Ochoco National Forest, east of Prineville, Oregon. I was two years old. My parents, Lee & Josephine Blevins, my five years old older sister Evelyn, and I had moved from the Blevins Ranch on the upper Ochoco, early that spring. We were living in a tent for the summer. A battery telephone (to the outside world) hung on a tree in front of the tent. A cabin had not yet been built on this location. Trails to and from this area were being established. Papa surveyed and did trail work on the early beginning, trails system. We as a family, that day had gone with Papa on a trip which was to take the better part of the week. We planned to camp each night, quite close to his work area, saving him many long hours of riding time each day, along the trail to and from Antler Station.*

## EARLY START
By:
V. June (Blevins) Collins

When a little less than a shaver,
Was just barely two years old,
I rode in front of my mother
In her saddle, almost bold.

Sister Evelyn rode on behind,
On Monte's back, rather well.
Felt like we're glued together,
For neither of us had ever fell.

That day we were way out on trail
From Antler Station, by the mile.
Parents, pack horse, dog and gear,
Head to tail, strung out single file.

Mid morning trail, became boggy.
Mud slurped and was getting deep.
Tracks grabbed a hold of hooves
Like demons, sucked down on feet.

Papa riding, and leading pack horse,
The three slowly crossed over log.
Stopped, waited, moved on slowly.
Was Monte's turn to cross the bog.

Monte, felt somewhat left behind.
Wanted to jump, not step across.
Mom gave him head, felt him bunch.
He just might give we three a toss.

She pulled, saying, "Take it easy."
He settled as he heard her voice.
Again, felt his jump intentions
As if he had, no other choice.

Time arrived for Monte's crossing.
With his load, he felt need to hop.
I flew from my mothers arms quickly
Onto log below, with thumping pop.

Rolled on down in front of Monte.
His front foot, above was aimed.
Mom hollered and pulled back hard.
He held, his mid position, framed.

Above my back, in apparent limbo.
Didn't dare let him go, because!
One front foot over log, in mud.
Other in limbo, on wavering pause.

Could have been all she wrote...
Dad made a wild dash and grab.
In relief, Monte allowed to cross.
Their grim position, close to sad.

Scared sounds, and soft whimpers
Came crying from trembling lips.
Mom felt up and down my legs a bit,
Found one break there, in left hip.

Both discussed their new situation
Agreed, leg right here, must be set.
Dad cut alders, whittled flat splints.
Disaster near felt but closely met.

Mom dug into pack *alforkuses.
The dish-towels found. Would do.
They pulled, straighten and wrap.
Somewhat unsure and both blue.

My complaining sounds became quiet.
Seems, had done a job... as a team.
Much work still lay ahead for both.
Yes, truly anything but a dream.

Papa Soon took off at a full gallop.
Packs were bounding along in tow.
Leading both horses, out behind,
For help, with very little slow.

Old dog, Dock, stayed by coaxing,
Had his own plan to catch up, too.
After those sounds of beating hooves,
He sneaked off, soon behind him flew.

Mom said, "Many items missing.
They'ed fallen out, along the way."
Packs flopping, as they ran in haste,
All scattered along trail, that day.

Finally Papa reached station, made a call,
From that phone anchored on the tree,
There beside tent, our home for summer.
Filled well, with mountain air, you see.

He put horse 'n pack horse into pasture.
Again, mounted Monte's sweating back.
Returned to meet we three stragglers,
Evelyn, Mom and her burden's pack

***Alforehass'** : A spanish word for the bags that hang on each side of the pack horse's saddle. Used extensively in early years of the West.. Soon it was destined to be corrupted, and called Alforkuses.

Mom said, "I was scared and so worried.
Could hear guttural moan of angry bulls."
In her fear, she spied a big monster rock
She'd boost me up, with sister's pulls.

Range bulls' bellers came closer, closer.
Made mom's heart skip beats, quick 'n fast.
Like haven meant, this specially rock found,
Was a much needed place to rest, at last.

Here to wait a while, yet still needed to go
On down gray lonely trail, feeling blue.
As on ahead, heard loud cracking of brush...
Lathered Monte, broke suddenly, into view.

Papa dismounted, boosted Mom back on
Off toward Antler, to ride and bags pack.
He walked... Me in his outstretched arms
And not upon his back.

Alex Donnelley was there, waiting in car,
By the time Papa had walked back in.
We're soon loaded up, and drive away,
Back down Summit Prairie road, again.

Past Ochoco Station to Blevins Ranch,
Still about twenty miles more, to town.
Dr. Belnap had come there to meet us,
Where on dining table, they lay me down.

Doctor, unwrapped my leg, felt about a bit,
And said, "He could not have done it better!
But closest x-ray was at The Dalles, Oregon."
There Mom 'n Coe would write many a letter.

Papa drove us down to Prineville that night,
Twenty more miles onto Redmond, and train.
Traversed the night, along Columbia River,
Arrived just before its dark began to wane.

Spent next six months there, at hospital.
Was wrapped in a cast, up to my arms.
Said, "stubbed about making new friends,
Plus turned on my best of charms."

They had to change size of cast twice.
Said I was a fast growing little squirt.
Seems I acted as if I had no problem,
For quickly mending, it didn't hurt.

My nurse's name, Mrs. Bottomiller.
A small ivory mirror was her gift.
It has served me many, many years,
Among treasured memories, as I sift.

Old Doc Gessner put on those casts.
Was a near body suit, for its day.
Was up my leg and around my body.
Voices whisper. Shall hear me say,

"Was start and beginning of horses,"
As told in the lines, above, I tell.
Horses have been my life's pleasures,
All my lifetime, have served me well.

Grandmother, Cora Blevins; Lee Blevins father; Awilda Josephine Blevins Mother;
Sister Evelyn, six years; V. June Blevins Collins, two years.

Photo by Isaac Madison Blevins (Grandfather)

1920, Antler Guard station in process of being built in its location south about seven miles, of Summit Prairie. Summit Prairie is between fifteen and twenty miles east of Ochoco Ranger Station which is twenty seven miles east of Prineville, Oregon.

Antler Station still was our home for the summer in a tent camp. Left to right, my Grandmother, Cora J. (Miller) Blevins; V. June Blevins, (four years); Mother's horse, **"Monte"**; Mother, Awilda Josephine (O'Kelley) Blevins; Mom's mother, my Grandmother, "Akio," Lydia Caroline (Elliott), O'Kelley; Papa, Lee Edward Blevins my dad; Evelyn Irene Blevins, my sister, (seven years.)

# MONTE

## By V. June Collins

*(By the way, our family said, "crick," not creek.)*

Monte was Mom's old saddle horse.
He was her pride and joy.
Monte still had one bad habit.
Was disgusting and did annoy.

Wherever you chose to tie him,
To a tree or to yonder fence,
He was bound to soon test it...
Dang, didn't make much sense.

He would then lay back on the rope
And give it a hard one, two, three.
Whip neck and head back and forth.
He knew this often set him free.

When the rope finally gave away,
Falling backward, he was loose.
This aggravated my Dad, for sure.
Said, "Needs a kick in his caboose."

He never seemed to run away when free.
Was just the thought of being tied.
But all the ropes that he had ruined...
Dad said, "Damn! Old Monte's hide."

Finally, a day came when out camping
Where strong trees near bank were few.
Was about fifteen feet from the crick.
Dad's planned idea grew and grew.

He tied Old Monte up to sturdy tree,
Between tree and the water's bank.
Threw up his hands and hollered loud...
Monte took the bait, onto haunches sank.

He lay back, gave a regular performance.
That special gleam shone in his eye.
Whipped old rope hard, back and forth.
Cinched rope tighter. It began to sigh.

Dad quickly gave axe a mighty swing
And cut rope with one fell chop.
Monte fell backwards in surprise,
With fast somersault and a plop.

My mom, in tears, loudly cried out,
"You've killed him!" above the melee.
"Break crazy habit or else," Dad remarked,
"He'll be a far better horse, you'll see."

He had landed ker-splash! In the water.
His surprise there was most great.
Finally, he floundered back to dry ground
In a wet, dripping, stumbling gait.

Yes, old Monte changed his fond habit.
Sold it forever, to stand and stay.
When first tied he'd tense, then give
As his water visions, began a replay.

Monte, it seems had lost old desires
To pull back, wherever he's tied.
Became a model kind of old horse
Just wearing his shiny sorrel, hide.

*This poem materialized after thinking about another happening during my early growing up years. Papa had now become the Ranger at Ochoco Ranger Station, where we were living. It was about 1922.*

## DAMPER SMART

By V. June Collins

**My dad left ranch in early days**
As guard when Ochoco's Forest new.
We camped and lived out in its arms
While I was still a tad of two.
**On summer job, we lived in a tent.**
Little family then quite small.
A battery telephone hung on a tree,
For you see, we lacked a wall.
**A few years later, he became Ranger**
To this out-post in a special time.
Yet, I wouldn't trade my growing years,
With anyone up or down the line.
**Mom ran switch-board there many years.**
Twenty-four hour service was for sure.
Sister Evelyn and I grew older, helped
Ring numbers and plug in callers more.
**I look back on many a happening.**
Soon my smiles turn into grin.
A thought about my mom, JO BLEVINS,
When she raised some hackles, then.
**Seems her stove at Ochoco Station**
Had given out in complete despair.
ALEX DONNELLEY brought another
That could stand a bit more wear.
**He unloaded it beside the kitchen.**
Mom was standing in, looking out.
She watched that fellow toil 'n slave
'Til all his patience most wore out.

**Seems stovepipe easily went together**
But that DAMPER just would not fit.
She watched him turn red in face
As his placement still, off a whit.
**He pushed 'n pulled without success**
Then started in to swear in vain.
Picked it up off of ground a bit,
And abruptly slammed it back again.
**Mom just knew she could help.**
A small suggestion just might do.
Surely he could use a pointer
Before all his gaskets blew.
**She quietly stepped from house 'n said,**
"SIR, If you would turn it this a-way,
It might slip right into place
Just might flip 'n tip 'n stay."
**He turned around with surly glare.**
Said, "Fix it! If so DAMN DAMPER SMART."
She ignored jab. Knelt softly down.
Started in taking it back apart.
**His eyes burned hot, on back of her neck.**
She felt red creeping to her face.
With dampers direction in reverse
It smoothly slid right into place
**He cleared his throat, picked up tools.**
Without a word, she returned to house.
With thoughts and smiles for many a day.
He'd just acted like a MACHO MOUSE.

Photo by Coe Blevins

"Pa," my Grandfather Ike Blevins, working his colt, "Midnight," while my Grandmother's dog, "Charlie", enjoys the fresh blanket of snow, too.

When this picture was taken by my Grandmother, I was 11 years of age and also watching the proceedings, or goings on.

(Charlie takes center stage, on page 17)

STATE OF OREGON

No. 1228

# CERTIFICATE OF REGISTRATION OF MARKS AND BRANDS

**This Is to Certify, That** I. M. BLEVINS

Residing at HOWARD

CROOK County, OREGON

has complied with the provisions of Chapter 33, General Laws of Oregon, passed at the Legislative Session of 1915, and has been awarded the exclusive right to use the fire brand or brands indicated and hereon described, on the particular location on the animal as indicated on the cut; and the ear and other flesh marks as hereon indicated and described on this certificate, to-wit:

HORSES—
BRANDED THUS: PB
ON LEFT STIFLE

NOTE—Brands must be placed on location given in this certificate.

RIGHT                LEFT

WATTLE
Draw line to, if used.

CATTLE—
BRANDED THUS: PB
ON LEFT HIP

Sheep _____ Other animals _____

Ear and flesh marks for cattle as indicated on ear and other part of cut as per diagram above and described as follows: Crop off left ear ans split in right ear.

Filed and recorded in the office of the State Veterinarian in Book " " " on the date of July 23, 1915.

STATE VETERINARIAN.

---

\* REFER TO PAGES 13-14 FOR MORE INFORMATION TO THIS PAGE.

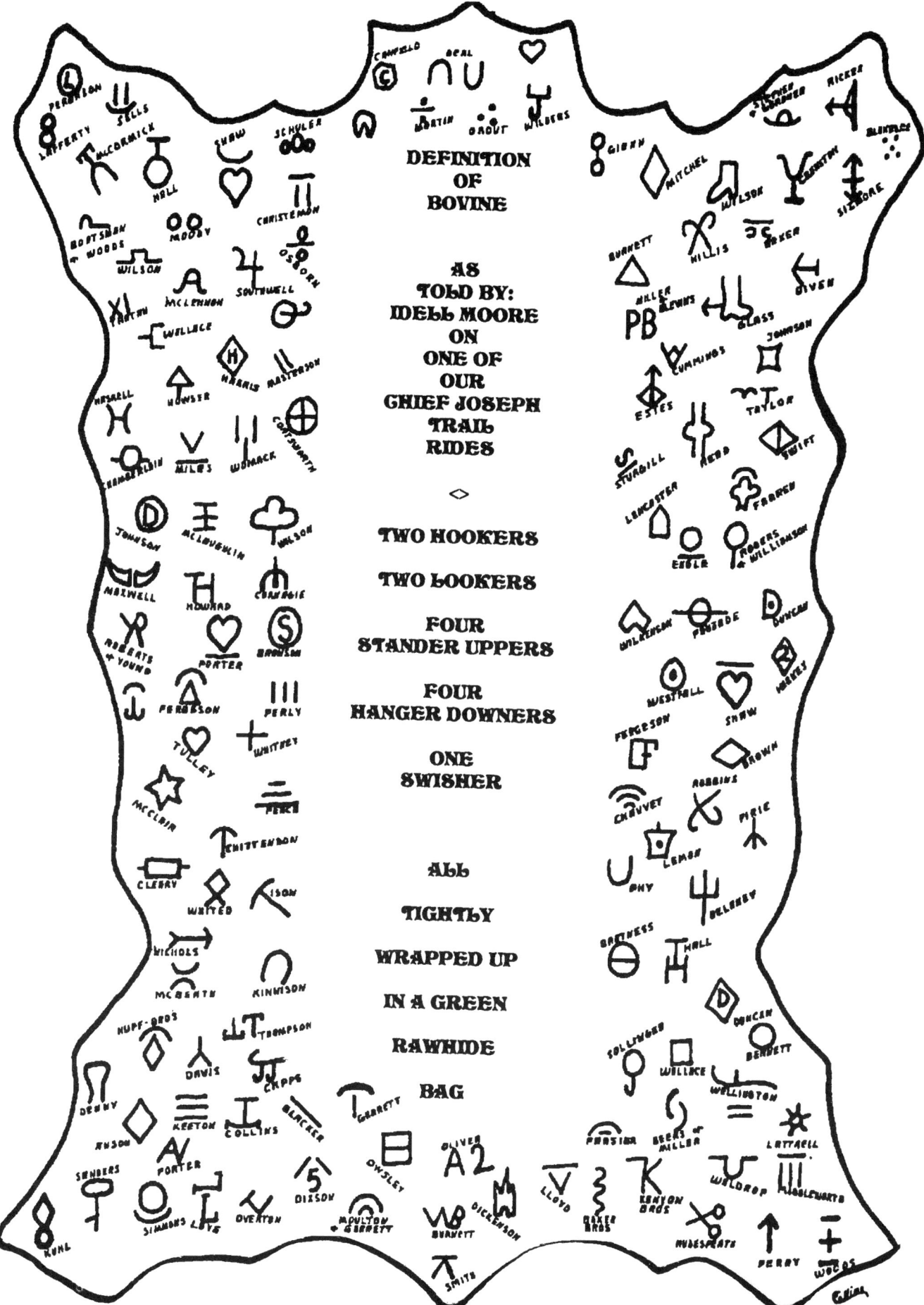

These brands are copied from my grandfather, Isaac. M. "Ike" Blevins' Brand Book, 1890, of Eastern Oregon Brands. PB was brand registered on left hip for cattle and left stifle on horses. Used by Penelton, & Ike, Blevins and S.W. Miller, Ike's father-in-law. (now caretaker of book, V. June Blevins Collins.)

# HAY-RACK CHORES
### (Dedication)

Listed around the border on page 13 are a few of the brands of 1890 in Eastern Oregon. These brands are in Grandfather, ISAAC M. BLEVINS', brand book. The brands represent a way of life. Among them is the PB brand of my Grandfather, and his Father PENELTON BLEVINS, my Great-Grandfather. The brand was also registered under MILLER & BLEVINS, including S. W. MILLER (Isaac's father in-law), my Great-Grandfather. S. W. MILLER was also, the first Assessor of Malhuer County, Oregon.

This poem is before the dawn of the "Haybaler's" existence when hay was manually forked onto wagons from the fields, hauled and unloaded at haystacks and barns for winter storage. Then, each day through the long winter months, the process was reversed and repeated, feeding the hay out to the livestock.

ISAAC M. "Ike" BLEVINS (my grandfather), was foreman of the MILLER & LUX CATTLE CO in Eastern Oregon for some time as a young man. He left there upon the death of his father, to take over the running of the home ranch on the upper Ochoco, 20 miles east of Prineville, where I grew up.

Their range lands consisted of all of Harney, Grant, Crook and Malhuer Counties in Oregon. Even in those days of leather, such a wide area could produce a few saddle sores on both horse and rider.

This poem I dedicate to my Grand and Great Fathers. The feed hay-racks and teams were driven by hardy souls, bundled with scarf and ear-mufflers to help endure the icicles that formed on mustaches in the stiff, biting cold which gnawed continuously at the warmth of courage.

All this to appease appetites in bovine hides, carrying brands once smoking hot, now cooled and worn in ragged woolly identity, like winter's shaggy overcoats.

*By V. June Collins*

# HAYRACK CHORES

By V. June Collins

Raw is day we're off and away
It's feeding time again.
The loaded wagon rolls along,
Out to the basin rim.
Hay drizzles off into the snow
Off the edges all around.
Wisps and stem skitter, fall
So softly to the ground.
Wheels in frozen snow complain
In loud and crispy moans.
The horses feet a rhythm beat
In squeaky high pitched tones.
It's music to the herds we feed.
They run hurriedly, along behind.
Grabbing mouthfuls every chance
Only breakfast on their mind.
Cold, and bellies mighty empty.
Loud bellers, let us know.
From open mouths, balls roll out
With puffs of breath that show.
Pitch it off from each side,
A fork full at a time.
They push, shove and boss away,
The young and timid kind.
After what seems an eternity,
As load scattered on the snow.
They menace one another still,
And trample along the row.
Snow mixes nicely among chaff,
At the bottom of each pile.
Cows enjoy snow cone dessert
In both group and single file.
A few short months, plates clean.
Each time we fork out the hay.
Thaws then turn white to brown
As snows melt and run away.

THE FOLLOWING POEM,
CALLED

# BRANDING TIME,

IS PRETTY MUCH SELF EXPLANATORY.

I ASK.
WERE YOU RAISED ON A CATTLE RANCH?

IF NOT,
PERHAPS THERE IS A NEED
TO CLARIFY THE WORD,
"OYSTERS."

MOUNTAIN
OR RANCH OYSTERS
ARE A DELICACY,

COLLECTED AT BRANDING TIME,
LATER
COOKED AND ENJOYED,
FRENCH FRIED,
AT A
SPECIAL MEAL
BY
RANCH FAMILIES.

THESE OYSTERS ARE DERIVED
FROM THE CASTRATION OF
BULL (MALE) CALVES...

THEREBY CHANGING THEIR MINDS
FROM HEIFERS
TO GRASS.
---
RANCH DOGS ARE ALSO
VERY FOND OF THE TASTE.
THEY AGGRESSIVELY WAIT
FOR A RAW DEAL!

*This happening took place at my Grandparents, Isaac and Coe (Miller) Blevins, ranch on the Upper Ochoco, east of Prineville, Oregon, one spring during branding time. I was about 12 years of age.*

BRANDING TIME

By V. June Collins

GRASSES greenin' in the pastures.
Yet, old wind is cool 'n sharp.
BRANDIN' FIRE NOW HEATIN' UP
With wood 'n smoke 'n spark.

HOT IRONS WAITING, in relay,
To cut sharp the burning hair.
ANOTHER YEAR'S crop of calves.
Familiar smells fill the air.

AN ANNUAL, COMMON CUSTOM
Is a Western Heritage and deed.
Happens each spring like ritual
Same as growing of the seed.

MOURNFUL BAWLS from mother cows,
All with worry for their young.
Calves answering back, EXCITED!
Like all other branding, has begun.

SEEMS ALWAYS to be an incident,
Some happening, to bring a smile.
As things don't go as scheduled
While some ropes MISS A MILE.

DOGS THINK oysters are a treat.
CHARLEY kept getting in the way.
Scolded to stay outside the fence.
Seems back inside, did stray.

GRANDMA COE finally had enough.
Grabbed rope to tie up this cur,
To keep him outside the fence.
Was one good thought, as it were.

ALL'S WELL, for quite some time.
Then he through fence did jump.
With not much rope to venture,
Sat in anxious, whining, lump.

Then mad mother cow WADED IN,
Started cleaning out the crew.
She did not stop after scatter
'Til She darn well, WAS THROUGH.

Charley used his DEEP LOUD BARK
To help each one reach a perch
As they nimbly, jumped for safety sake,
For ALTITUDES, in speedy lurch.

Charley then, WAS NEXT IN LINE
Though he didn't know, right then.
with that gol-darned old rope,
It soon would do him in.

HE TRIED FAST, To leave the country!
Rope it stopped him real fast.
OLD COW was baring down on him,
Her chance to do him in, AT LAST!

SHE BAWLED 'N snuffed, LOUD!
Put that fur ball in rotation.
She was really one mad old cow,
BLOWED SNOT all over creation.

His mind said,"GO WEST MY BOY!"
As rope again, came to sudden end.
Old cow was right behind him,
To his rear end, SHE DID ATTEND.

She gave a heave, TOSSED HIM HIGH!
Into air he was turning loop.
YELPIN' LOUD from her tussle.
Missing hide could not recoup.

SHE again circled brandin' fire.
Caught old Charley 'n his rope.
HE SAILED ABOVE HER HEAD A BIT.
At her mercy, he tried to cope.

When he came to that ropes end,
Out from under him she dashed.
Again he started back to earth,
HOLLERIN' LOUDLY AS HE CRASHED!

Rope had reached its limit.
LIKE A SLING SHOT COMING DOWN.
Right into the burning embers.
We sat watching, all around.

As gravity then took over,
Headin' down, CAME MIGHTY FAST.
Not to be a three point landing.
HIS DOOM WAS THEREBY CAST.

He landed in the branding fire.
The WOOD 'N COALS DID SCATTER!
HIS LEGS WERE SPINNING CIRCLES!
He did not stay long for chatter.

HE SCRAMBLED OVER TOP OF FENCE!
Was sure head'n for his escape.
Our message he had plum ignored
'TIL OLD BOSSY CHANGED HIS SHAPE!

She again circled around the fence,
Checkin' those up on their roost.
Showed that she's plum willing
TO GIVE EACH ANOTHER BOOST!

After ALL THE DUST HAD SETTLED
And crew climbed down from fence,
They rekindled fire, just a bit,
Heaved a sigh from all suspense.

Then we again sure had a laugh
At OLD CHARLEY DOG'S expense.
For he, the rest of day, stayed put,
Outside that brandin' fence.

THROUGH YEARS, he's not forgotten.
Into conversations, didn't tire.
His notoriety sure made rounds, of
How "OLD CHARLEY STOKED THE FIRE!"

Photo By V. June Collins

*This story was related to us, years later, by our dear, long-time friend, Rue Freeman. Even then, he got embarrassed all over again, as he related the happening. We, in sympathy, of course, laughed and cried as he told it.*

## LONG SHIRT TAILS

By V. June Collins

This is a long-tailed, short story
Of a special friend along the line.
He told a tale of his very first job,
When not everything, was going fine.

Long before Invironmental Wackos,
Would shudder from just the thought.
Thinking, all that comes naturally,
Should forever, almost be forgot.

He was then a man, of just fifteen years,
Dressed in a long-tailed, old plaid shirt.
Thought he was pretty much accepted,
Like others covered with dust and dirt.

Seems this young fellow way back then,
Had many duties, he still never shirked.
Yon' bushes being their only facilities...
Out in logging woods where he worked.

   Finally old noon hour came, at last,
   Each on hillside, lounged and sat.
   Some on logs, ground and stumps,
   Eating lunch, amongst some chat.

   Most likely, was just shootin' bull,
   For their day, had been going well.
   My friend's duty-call, came calling,
   And he had to find a bush, pell-mell.

Long-tailed shirt, was something new,
And, quick like, had come to grief.
And suddenly proved his undoing
   Sitting there squatted, in relief.

His mind felt scrambled, in a jumble,
What ever could or should he do?
Without shirt, if he went back to work?
Crew would sure have, one hoop-tee-do.

He could not ever let them know.
Felt it might be better, should he die.
Never could he ever, to live it down,
Would be their conversation high.

Another thought emerged, some better.
If he was lucky, it just might work.
He could get along without shirt-tail,
His frown turned into, an almost smirk.

Sure, this way he could go back to work,
Avoid disgrace, that was comin' fast.
As last resort, pulled out pocket-knife
And cut off that dreadful blast.

His face shown red with worry still,
Like a thief, his guilt almost shown.
He prayed to God, his very own secret,
Would not somehow, become known.

Rest of workers were getting busy
He could almost hear his silence throb.
He buried that troophy in the hillside
And nonchantly, sauntered back to job.

Many long years went painfully by,
Before he repeated his lowly tale.
For he had forever, learned a lesson
Keep guarded eye, on old shirt tail.

Photo By Isaac Blevins

*Our young Shepherd ranch dog, Sprout, still much a pup, was on his first cattle drive to the summer range. He had not yet learned, as did the older dogs, to make himself scarce where bees and yellow jackets are concerned.*

## SPROUT
### (A Young Dog)

Sprout, took on a gob of stings
With an angry bunch of jackets.
Tussle soon got out of hand
With yelping sound 'n racket.

His hair was long, took some time
Before they backed down to his hide.
Heat quick then turned up to high
With stinging both far 'n wide.

His human friends deserted him
Was left all alone to rattle.
He snapped, snarled, biting fast,
Still more arrived for battle.

At high speed, in time took off,
Leaving Bee Country far behind.
Only stops, were to dislodge a few
Seems ten thousand more assigned.

Finally in a heap lay, in exhaustion,
His aching pains most searing.
He chewed, and licked for relief...
His ears had stopped their hearing.

His eyes could no longer see
Small slits, they too, did close.
He lay in whimpering misery,
Whining pain, as he arose.

Day wore on, into cold of night
Seemed more dead than alive.
Welted body, pulsed and throbbed,
In his struggle now, to survive.

Eyes and ears were lost to him.
His sniffing nose, most numb.
This helpless lump lay crying,
In state, both deaf and dumb.

Three long days and three nights
He was finally given up as lost.
A young black shepherd cow dog,
Felt memory must accept the cost.

It was on eve of number four
Away long past the afternoon.
Approached a bedraggled creature,
Staggering, taking lots of room.

His head looked like water bucket
Still near half again its size.
A pitiful dog in need of comfort,
This specimen, would take no prize.

A Big Heart, brought him through,
He would reign in storm and strife.
Sprout, became a cow dog supreme,
An old King Pin, the rest of life.

*This poem I wrote of a period in my life when about thirteen years of age. I call it*

### JIM
### By V. June Collins

My sister had an unbroken filly
We could not so utilize and ride.
When a man and daughter drove along
Pulled out, stopped by road's side.

They said horse they're leading
Built too light to pull in collar.
He'd tried, it seems, and sores made.
He was now lead behind, to foller.

Said, "Sure he's broke to ride.
Why, he's even been raced a bit."
So trade soon made by Grandad, Pa,
That seemed fair 'n square to fit.

Pa said was now my job to doctor
With sulfur and bacon grease.
To water, feed, brush his coat...
Permission to ride he'd later release.

He was a Chestnut from head to toe.
Was I thought a flashy fellow.
He shook his head 'n pranced about.
Each time he seemed more mellow.

Days rolled by, then some months.
Finely hair grew in with bits of white.
I brushed, cleaned and shoveled out
As dreamed astride, would soon alight.

Finally waited for, spring day arrived
So I now saddled him with pride.
I rode him around 'n around corral
As he reined with ease of guide.

At end of week, feeling confident,
Asked to ride a few miles down road
To neighbors, on below on creek.
Of girl friend's place, abode.

I put a snaffle on my bridle
To treat him soft and kind.
Pa then questioned my ability
To control, should he unwind.

But I answered back, "He's O.K!"
Then traveled on through trees.
Soon came to upper pasture gate
Which he sidled up to, with ease.

Riding with *surcingle 'n saddle pad.
He maneuvered to open 'n shut gate.
Then trotted securely along in field
With no need to stop or hesitate.

I visited across fence a spell.
My friend liked Jim's shiny view.
Time then came to return again
So back-tracked same way too.

Had gone only a short distance
When I kicked him on into a lope.
He smoothly dashed across field
Jumping ditches along the slope.

---

***Surcingle**: A strap we extended and buckled around the girth of the horse, most often over the top of blanket or saddle pad., which prevented us from getting our legs and clothing wet, sweaty, and covered with hair, from the horse. Plus grasp on to when needed, to keep from falling off horse.

Decided then should pull him up
As gate seemed fast closing in.
But I found each time I pulled back
He only added more speed within.

I knew that he could really jump.
This vision sure did not set well.
Arms now weary from pulling back
As we're dashing on pell-mell!

Now my mind was sure made up
When he cleared that thar gate.
A fact that we'd part company
And I wouldn't have long to wait.

I didn't shut my eyes right then
Though I knew the jig was up.
Instead, Jim slammed on all four brakes
Right then, with rupp! rupp! rupp!

I was so surprised, yet relieved,
I closed both eyes in prayer.
Slowly opened up that swingin' gate
To other side, still feeling grayer.

Just walked Jim the rest of way.
Then put him back into his stall.
Hereafter rode That Old Dude
With spade I'd left hanging on the wall.

I rode him many time thereafter.
Each time he'd be waiting for a race,
Kind you start in the opposite direction,
Wheel, and dash to hit your pace.

Aproximately, 1922.                                    Photo By Isaac M. Blevins

Cora Jane (Miller) Blevins (my grandmother) holding a young horse and mare for a picture of the **foal, the 1/2 Clydesdale colt, Mike.** With them are two spotted hound dogs, Dill & Pickles and Pink, the (black) dog. Dit, is the (Tanish-brindle) dog in front of the picture. **Ranch house and barn in the middle ground.** Lookout Mountain can be seen in the far back ground.

This Blevins place was homesteaded by Penelton Blevins, and his wife, Julia Ann Welch, in 1871, about the same time Prineville, Oregon was becoming a town. Isaac Madison was nine years of age when his parents moved to Wasco County, (now Crook County) to establish themselves a home, 20 miles up the Ochoco from Prineville.

As a young man, Isaac was Foreman for Miller and Lux Outfit, in the Malhuer country of Harney County. In 1906 his father died from blood poisoning, after a scratch on his hand from a barb-wire fence.

Isaac, at that time took over the running of Ochoco Ranch. His mother, Julia Ann, also homesteaded an adjoining piece of land after the death of her husband, Penn. This made a total of 880 acres, plus available lease land. He had a life-time lease for summer range land on Lookout Mountain. Cattle were driven there each spring. Four generations of hard times and good times. Ended upon Isaac's death in 1931. But, I still wouldn't trade my childhood with any one.

*This poem is of a happening in my early life. During the time when loose hay was stacked into barns and stacks with teams of horses, and not baled.*

## MIKE
### (A Clydesdale)

### By V. June Collins

Summer's haying had come to end
Teams now, had earned their rest.
Some grazed out in pastures,
Others turned to hills with zest.

During days they made their rounds.
As they came in sight we noted tally.
Sometimes on steep terrain, far away.
Other times, down near the valley.

That day arrived, one horse missing.
Granddad and I saddle up, a horse.
With need to check this water-shed,
Each ridge and slope of course.

Found Mike absent. Aroused a dread.
We rode along with a peeled eye.
The day wore on, sun bearing hot...
Chicken Hawks circled in the sky.

At Box Springs stopped for drink.
Took a sandwich from our sack.
Ate, still felt uneasy like...
Soon back on horse's back.

Around two, we topped final ridge.
Soon arrived at drift fence gate.
Mike stood near, front feet in wire.
We shuddered, had arrived too late.

Mike whinnied as he heard us coming,
With welcome thoughts. Alas, helps came!
Though too late now. He'd never know.
Beyond our grasp, our sadness reigned.

He was standing on back of *pasterns.
Had worried and sawed them through.
His tendons snapped and severed...
Beyond, freedoms frantic efforts, view.

His long struggling tries, so apparent.
The ground between posts were plowed.
With barb-wire's wicked, stubborn way...
His escape from grasp was not allowed.

He now stood patient, 'til each foot
Was lifted out and again, set free.
His eyes said, "All would be well."
But that could never, never, be!

Why taken so early to Horse Heaven?
Leaving others that habits gall.
Why an honest work horse so chosen?
Mike pulled willingly 'n gave his all.

Tears filled both our eyes.
Dread now filled our wills.
Rifle taken down from scabbard.
A shot rang out through hills.

The ride back home was only silent.
A special friend destroyed, now gone.
This Gentle Giant was no more.
Still, a deed meant right, felt wrong.

***Pasterns**: Above the hoof, like the ankle or wrist part of horses foot.

*Previously Published: 1992, by Siskiyou Writing Club, in Collected Works of Siskiyou Poets; In 1999, Songs Of The Siskiyou's, by Living Gold Press.*

## VIRGINIA JOSEPHINE
### (a cow)

WE WERE YET GROWING SPROUTS.
That was quite some time ago.
Yes, many things have changed.
I shall up and tell you so!

Old milk cows were then roped
From out of our cattle herd.
Tied and milked, to gentle.
Her BAWLS 'n BELLERS HEARD.

A SPECIAL OLD COW. A DURHAM CROSS.
Brought to feed the Blevins' Boss.
His family all drank their fill.
She lacked a name. So, to fill bill...

Sister, Evelyn, a name volunteered.
VIRGINIA JOSEPHINE! Stuck and adhered.
To shout this name took a very long time.
Buckets kicked over like assembly line.

Mamma, JOSEPHINE, was especially meant.
Baby sister VIRGINIA, most heaven sent.
Name wore like bell, called with glee.
DAD GUFFAWED LOUD his HAW 'n HEE! HEE!

Yet, time has a way of calming us all.
Soon milked her in corral, not in stall.
She fast became reconciled to this tribe.
We'd milk twice daily, then could imbibe.

MY AUNT THEN CAME TO VISIT one day.
It changed old V. J.'s winning way.
V. J. took one look at that thar doll,
LOWERED HER HEAD 'N BEGAN TO BAWL.

The dirt did rattle against the barn.
SHE PAWED 'N SNUFFED, 'N TRIED TO WARN.
Aunt Mabel across corral still came.
Thinking old V. J. was playing game.

SOON V. J. DOWNED HER HEAD IN CONTEMPT.
Sure scared Aunt Mabel in her attempt!
At bottom of fence a hole did appear.
AUNT MABEL DOVE THROUGH! UP TO HER REAR.

Was hole the dog used to make his escape
When old bossy tried to change his shape.
Aunt Mabel was stuck at the trailing end.
SHE SQUEALED 'N KICKED WITHOUT PRETEND!

OLD V. J. STOPPED SHORT, BLOWED THE AIR!
Snortin' wide-eyed, about the whole affair.
Cautiously, Mabel backed herself out,
Amidst much ribbing, laughter 'n shout.

Could have no more fun at her expense
As thereafter stayed outside of fence.
Years went by, VIRGINIA JOSEPHINE a pet,
Became THE BEST OLD COW you ever met.

Tho' at milking time, she'd hide in brush.
WE'D SIC OLD DOG, HE'D HEAL WITH A RUSH!
She'd jump 'n kick from his bite 'n nip.
Her bell tinkle. We'd through willows slip.

IT WAS HIDE 'N SEEK FOR EVELYN 'N I
And OLD DOG SOCKS, who was our spy.
It got to be, sorta, a regular game,
For each milking was much the same.

Photo by V. June Collins

If only fences and buildings could talk. Great stories they would tell, and what good visits we would have.

Photo by V. June Collins

This old fence shows it has lead a double life with a long history. The oval holes apparent, where in boards it was once, swathed. Regal it must have stood. Starch stiff, dressed like in a tuxedo and proudly guarding its special family domain.

Today it also shows the mixture of different kinds of wire, still intent on controlling different sized livestock. With old age, still determined to do its necessary job. Between awake and asleep the struggle goes on.

# FENCES
## By V. June Collins

Chopped, sawed, split, from forest tree,
Staunch posts of fences like sentinels be.
Planted in earth, stand erect in ground,
Some tilt, stare and star-gaze around.

For some, what an effort it is to stand
As far distant rows criss-cross land.
Running over hill, down into gullies deep
While others stand still, as if asleep.

When drifts get deep and pile up high
Snow caps slouch down and cover eye.
Their backs are turned upon the wind.
Still never, do you see them bend.

Lined up in queues to where ever sent
Though alone and bleak, appear content.
Swathed in wire, for so many needs.
Different designs, makes and breeds.

Gnarly old wire, with barbs like thorn
Cut gashes deep, into trees deform.
Wicked old wire, from out of past
Takes different forms, was built to last.

More than hundred years, is still around.
Wired in with new, buried under ground.
As barbs become entangled in the bush
Some lean 'n pull, others shove 'n push.

For in its stubborn, and silent way
Soon prods those that don't obey.
It encloses grass, and gathers up land,
Reaches prairies with an outstretched hand.

Photo by V. June Collins

Fence along the road at the old Malloy Place, northeast of Montague in Shasta Valley, Siskiyou County, California.

Across many a mile, clear out of sight
With wrath-some vigor and quiet might.
Takes out revenge on such gentle folk
Fighting back hard when cut or broke.

It springs, leaps away, asserts its right,
Coils in anger and twists in delight.
Man and beast, in surprise it entangles
With drooping strands among brambles.

Like lurking snakes hid in the grass,
Waits quiet, unseen, until you pass.
Patiently awaits its change of luck
'Til alas, another blow is struck.

Furiously jabs, cuts, wraps around,
Writhes in new place upon the ground.
Old fence with past, whose secret's out
Again stands silent, in anger you shout.

Superior in strength, with life lived long.
Dumb beyond reason, lies silently, strong.
Those wise old fences, don't seem to care
When discarded, 'n stripped naked and bare.

Beginning of fencing, where e'er you look.
Stories could tell, would fill many a book.
So now the collectors are taking their toll
From old line fences, down to old water hole.

With oohs! and aahs! for each special kind.
An 18" strand's rarity is like silver you find.
Another way of life takes over our earth.
Another fond hobby has inevitable rebirth.

Photo By V. June Collins

This four wire fence, is shown in the fall, after wires have been dropped from fence posts, up in the high country, and ready for winter's deep snows. It's far easier to put unbroken wires back on fence posts come spring, than to repair broken wire breaks.

This alternative solution shown in the above photo, is used to keep the weight of snow from breaking fence wires, during the deep snow of winter because snow melts from underneath, next to the ground, first. The snows laden wires hang heavier, as the snows melt, and soon becomes unable to support the weight and stress, as wires are pushed downward, with such intense pressure, it can stretch no more and wires break. When spring comes, man is forced, again, to mend the fence.

On range land drift fences, this method is often used. Each fence post has four sets of two staples, in pairs, driven equal distant into the fencing side of each post. A loose staple is then dropped through in front of the wire used as a lock. Upon the removal of this lock staple from the two staples, it allows you to remove the wire from the post, and drop the wire to the ground. You place the removable staples back into the former position for the winter. Come spring again, the lock staple is removed, to place the strand of wire back between each two staples, in respective places, dropping the loose staple back in front of the wire, to hold the wires in place on the post, for the summer.

Photo By V. June Collins

Like an artists wild depictions, see cloud faces of every kind.

*Written of a period in my life when I was about 14 years of age. I was checking drift fence with Grandad, Pa, Isaac M. Blevins, during a time my sister and I spent much time helping our Grandparents with needed chores.*

### FENCE FIXIN'

By V. June Collins

Was working his way along fence
Then he stopped to fix a break.
Stepped back on to his horse
Soon be nearing saddle's gate.

I fixed my last break in the wire
And heaved a thankful sigh.
Upon this ridge we're to meet.
Could both daydream at sky.

I lay down on back, in the grass
As Jungles, grazed near by.
Watched floating, moving clouds
Drifting Eastward in the sky.

Like an artist's wild depiction's
Seeking someone's open mind.
Eyes 'n mind viewed many faces
Cloud shapes, of every kind.

Heard Jungles, softly whinny
In a low, like muffled sound.
I then raised my gaze a bit
Just a ways, above the ground.

Up out of deep draw, he came
A ways off down hill, below.
Granddad, Pa, other fence fixer
Still traveling rather slow.

He was working way along fence
Then stopped to fix a break.
Stepped back on to his horse
Soon will be nearing gate.

Upon this ridge we were to meet.
Would both daydream, at sky.
Is like medicine for the soul
Each exercising mind 'n eye.

Rest here, well earned today
Have little else in plan.
Fold down in relaxing pose
Both this kid, and weary man.

Time will become our very own
A refreshing, deliberate goal.
Individual thoughts materialize,
While resting both body 'n soul

Photo By V. June Collins

Rail Corrals, at Barnum Springs, near the base of Sheep Rock in Shasta Valley, and Siskiyou County California.

Photo By Jerry Collins

Agnes, Wally, Stell, Ernie Lemos and June on Tango Riding for cattle, before branding time, in hills above Copco Lake.

*Tango, another of life's games of chance, I wouldn't have missed for the world.*

### TANGO

By V. June Collins

*1947*
Charlie Page was an old gambler
In Yreka, that played the game.
One night he fell heir to a packstring
Plus horses, several just the same.

We were asked a short time later
To go hunting on Mountain of Cottonwood.
All would be riding some of these horses,
From his winnings, it was understood.

My mount for that day's encounter
Was Buckskin, tied 'n standing there.
A two-year-old, that appeared gentle.
She was a tall and willowy mare.

I put my gun down in the scabbard.
With quite some stretch, was aboard.
Her rein could stand some improvement
Later, today's events would record.

We all started off, single file,
Up steep ridges, across into draws.
'Til finally topped a high overlook...
Where again, horses blow 'n pause.

Soon had stations, each assigned,
Some to make stands, others drive.
While beating brush in the process,
Old buck's doom, just might arrive.

It seems this morn my lot is dog!
Myself and this yellow mare.
From up on top path looked clear
But up there we were not aware.

Horn of saddle kept hanging up.
Mare calmly offered no stampede.
I'd unhook and scramble farther,
A few yards, only, to succeed.

Reached thick overlay on ahead.
Forced to my knees as I crawled.
Again looked back at little mare,
And in dismay, most appalled.

She on her knees, was close behind me,
Working her way among brambles too.
WOW!--- Talk about HORSE SENSE!
Of this young gal, I will say to you!

I for sure now, was sold on her.
Was wishing only, I could buy.
For the small jingles in our pockets,
I feared, was far to little, to apply.

You see, were yet young married folk
That on a tight budget did exist.
One hundred was all of the currency
We could scrape up, into our fist.

It seemed Charlie asked One fifty,
So concluded, was just not meant.
That I would ever get to own her
My desire, to soon, curbed 'n bent.

A long year went by, heard phone ring,
Charlie voice, was at the other end.
He said, "If you still want that mare?
She's yours?" "My case I here amend."

"It was to that fool, I'd promised her."
"He wanted me to throw in my dog, too."
"This straw has broken the camels back..."
"Has changed my mind, from him to you."

Elated I waited for Jerry's return home.
In short time, from Dunsmuir did travel.
*Hove into Henley, pulling old horse trailer,
Where our plans started in, to unravel.


* **Hove in:** Arrived, drove in.

We knocked at door, a fool appeared.
His gun-belt strapped, onto his hip.
 Said he, "No way! Can you have mare!"
"You've just wasted your time, 'n trip.

Was back to Yreka town, we all went.
Talked both to Charlie Page and Sheriff.
They soon had path, preparedly, clear,
Without fears, more cost, or tariff.

We lost little time, in getting on back.
Loaded Tango into trailer, real fast.
Yellow mare would soon now become...
My very special friend, at last.

We hauled her on back to Cantara Loop.
There, at a barn and pasture we rent.
Put her with horses Tom, Jerry 'n Jeep,
'Til later on, back to Yreka were sent.

Pleasure from my Buckskin mare
Lasted more than twenty years.
Need I say, Upon her passing
Eyes 'n hearts filled with tears.

She was one super mountain horse,
Calm and honest, most hard to beat.
Still, fond void lasts, inside my heart
Though many others, I would meet.

They say it takes two to Tango.
With this phrase, I have no doubt.
She sure filled bill, rated as special...
My Buckskin mare! - My Super Mount!

Photo By V. June Collins

NOON HOUR REPRIEVE

"Painting"

Done by palette knife only

1961

By V. June Collins

*This poem came into being from a painting I was doing with palette knife, in oil of an old Jean Jacket and Cowboy hat hanging from a nail. While painting I kept listening, in memory, to the sounds that filled my ears, during many lunch times at the old ranch house. Hungry haying and branding crews were fed. I could almost hear old Jean Jacket talking about...*

## NOON HOUR REPRIEVE

By V. June Collins

With a shrug and a plop
I'm hung on the wall.
Pushed gladly aside
By another lunch-hour call.

Hanging on beneath my hat,
I look out and around.
Watch his face wash clean
From black as the ground.

Hair doused in water,
Quickly combs, slicks it back.
Casually saunters on in
For that ready, hot snack.

I hear sharp tinkle of dishes
And utensils click.
Familiar soft chuckles
Among laughs, loud and quick.

Foods disappear
As more helpings they take.
Stuffed by dessert,
Still cutting more cake.

Sighs, groans. So full.
The push back of chair.
From the table staggers,
Just needing some air.

They drape themselves loosely
On old porch so shady.
Snooze, shoot bull,
Tell a few which are jadey.

Yes, I enjoy patiently
The old noon hour lull.
Not ever real fancy,
But neither is it dull.

That gusty old breeze
Made my hat do a flip,
Slid down, right across
open eyes, to my lip.

Now, how is a guy
Expected to stay awake
When stopped from watching,
For goodness sake.

My memory tells me how
They look, lounge and lay.
For I watch over them,
Smiling, most every day.

I'm sure and I know
When they start back to work.
Before I'm dragged quickly
Off that nail with a jerk.

I'll hear them teasing
The New One, for sure.
Rib him hard during duties
And for many a chore.

"Hurry over and bring me
A left-handed monkey wrench."
And, "Go ask the horse
The left or right of a cinch."

Think soon he'll be accepted,
Become one of the boys.
Been one rugged struggle,
Absorbing all of their noise.

Well, it's again time to take me
Back out in the sun and, Pardner,
Finish up those critters
On this ranch you run.

Written while painting this picture, by same name
in pastels, in 1967 - vjc

DISTANT WHISPERS

By V. June Collins


Distant Whispers on the prairie echoed softly all around
To a lonely vigil-keeping, as the sands of time run down.
He rode off in the distance looking for that fresh new home.
To settle down, till the ground with fields of rich black loam.
Sun broke o'er a Mountain top like a beacon on a hill.
Bathed the valley in sunshine and on water that'd run a mill.

He'd seen this place long ago and knew t'was meant for him.
As now that she had promised had headed out around the bend.
He'd have to stay and work a spell. They'd soon own that special spot.
A large and mighty kingdom grows from this, their granted plot.
Hoof beats sounded muffled, as grew faint and far away.
Dust upon horizon gold, lingered on at break of day.
Out of reach so far away only numbness left behind.
Their calls of love so near, for-ever to be entwined.
At the close of every evening before night could shut the door
She walked alone in waiting and prayed for them once more.
Days grew long, weeks rolled by, months dragged on, no end.
He would return he'd promised but no letters did he send.
On through lonesome nights he's out of sight and hearing.
Loneliness cries aloud, with pangs of empty searing.
Her longing lingers in each look, lasts on into the gloaming.
Heart stood still, skipped a beat, 'Twas - buffalo herds a roaming.
Waiting, she'd made a promise, when again he rode in view.
He'd not go forth without her for his wife she'd be, she knew.
Each setting sun she takes her place on the break of that little hill.
To pray and wish him homing safe with a strong and mighty will.
She knew sure as this night came, so long they both had waited.
Before the sun could rise again They together, would be mated.
Distant Whispers started calling through the valley's every cord.
Soon she saw his image crossing through the waters at the ford.
So slowly he rode toward her. In exhausted steps so slow.
Could he be a double vision? She stood still and looked below.
Could she wait a little longer? Then the moon broke from a cloud.
He too could see her standing and called out her name aloud.
He lunged out of the saddle From the back of weary horse.
Stumbled running up the hill, a straight and steady course.
She met him, hands outstretched amid cries of joy and bliss.
He enfolded her into his arms fast smothered in their kiss.
At last the wait was over. Together they're as one!
Off and starting life anew. In their valley of the sun.

# WICKED WIRE OF THE WEST

By V. June Collins

When
Space is no problem, can roam at our will.
Time seems like forever, but never stands still.
Space becomes crowded, greed takes a hand.
Start putting up fences, on this giant of land.

Twists 'n cramps freedom so completely enjoyed.
And makes many beings, especially annoyed.
Fences are strung in gullies and brake.
All living through them, believers do make.

Unaware, with speed, 'tis hit before seen,
Damage is done... It's wicked and mean!
It kills and maims, raw edges saw deep.
In solid defiant rage, still its privacys, keep.

I'm chasing old Bawly, down out of brush
Toward valley's green grasses, below, so lush.
She cuts back sharply, disappears into thicket.
Charging, we come down, like tied to a picket.

Instant whine of wire screamed out, in revenge!
Echoed after ol' Bawly! 'Twas horror's wild twinge!
Riding Old TATERS, we together, come down!
In a tangle of flesh, as he's up-ended, on ground.

Taters struggles for freedom, in grunts, groans loud.
Frantic eruption of hooves, ground becomes plowed.
Wild struggle goes on, as wire lashes deeper.
Hill-side slants away, down in gully, far steeper.

Everything go black, pain dims, goes away.
Again, suddenly returns, my view is a sway.
As try to focus my eyes, in struggle to see,
Pain welted a message! So, alive I must be.

Taters is seen standing, head near the ground.
Relieved, he's not gasping or making a sound.
Vision becomes clearer, he looks like a steak!
Lord he's a mess! What a beating to take!

Old Taters, for me, would give it his all.
Without hesitation, or how great, the fall.
Old Bawly, had hit first, still lay in a heap.
Left tripper's for Taters, for flip, 'n repeat.

Her direction diverted, force broke screeching wire.
Slammed base of sentinel tree, with no plan to retire!
Head wedged 'neath big root, body twisted over, in vain.
She'd drawn card, placed bet, in bull-headed disdain.

Old Bawly, here, had met her sad end.
Her black hide, powered in violence.
Independence she'd chosen to dish out.
Suddenly left her, independently, in silence.

Ol' Taters stood bloody, sawed clean to the bone.
Cutting wire had latched on as flipped me out alone.
My chaps were a mess, much hide it was gone.
Thankful, ripping old wire hadn't stayed long.

As wire broke away, I'd catapulted into space.
All things come down! Glad 'twas not on my face!
Down hillside I slid, flame 'n smoke smothered.
The rear of my chaps left a lot to be covered.

Taters' wounds real nasty, with care, will heal.
I shan't be sitting for some time, we feel.
Years have gone by, barbwire still takes its toll.
Loathsome, old *barbwire with horrors its goal.

It will last 'til we die, reflecting back into view.
For barbwire often, hated, by me!
Yes, and old TATERS, too!

*__Barbed Wire:__ *So its correct, it's still barbwire to me!*

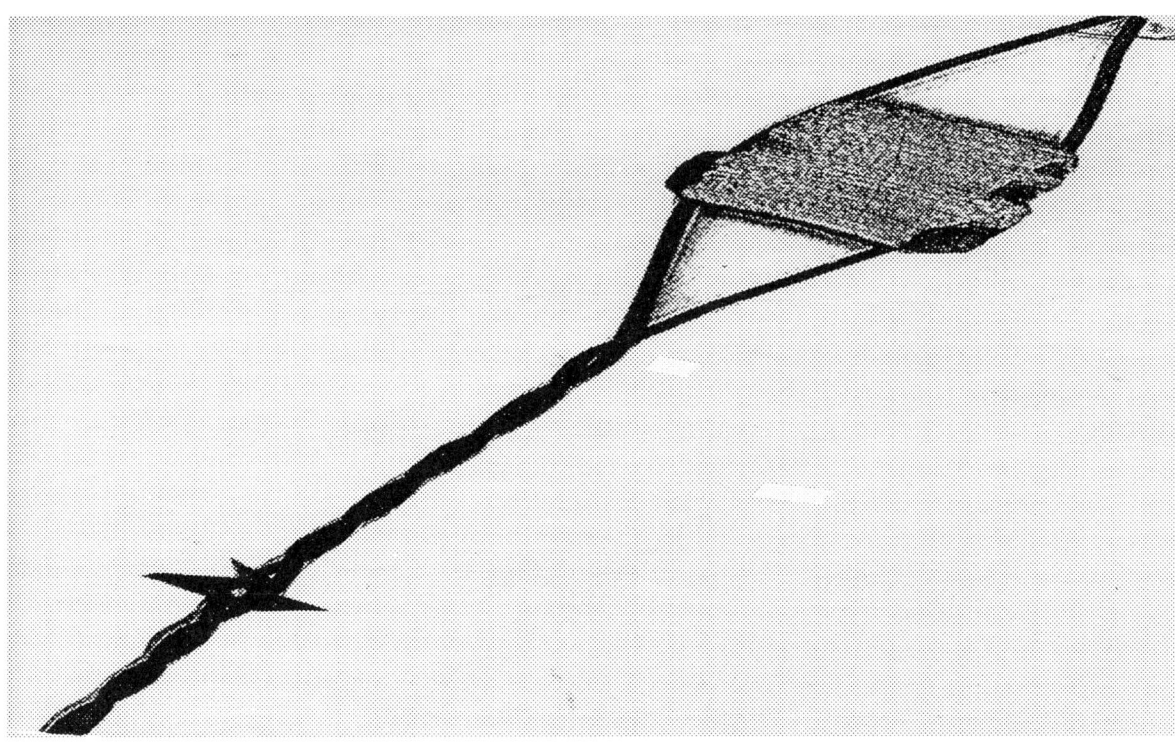

  This piece of barbwire . It was made by H.B. Scutts, and designated as Wooden Block, Barbwire, It was registered at the U.S. Patent office in 1880. The addition of this wooden block was so designed, with the intent to make fence wire more visible to live stock, and reduce its toll, barbwire had on all of those not yet, alert, to its damaging existence.
This rare piece shown is from my small collection, and was given to me by Keith Severns' 1st Cousin Hatasu Olsen, and her husband Leo, of Blackfoot, Idaho. He told me it came from the Shrodle Ranch near by.
  For a number of years I collected many of these 18" length pieces of barbwire, with much enthusiasm. Collectors of Barbwire are called Barbarians. (So I guess I are one. Maybe just a watchful, has been. V.J.C.)

Photo By V. June Collins

Where stubborn determined barbwire meets and deforms The Locust Tree, at a corner in the fence line. Up the Klamath River, above Topsy Grade on the Old Raymond Place.

Photo By V. June Collins

Those remembered views, between the ears of your horse, as only he will tell you. More than 1500 miles on the back of "Blue."

*I awakened at three one morning with the lines of the second verse steadily repeating to my sleepy mind, like aloud. I lay in thought awhile, not wanting to get up, yet knowing by morning only a memory would linger. In the dark, I soon started scribbling onto a pad, marking stops of each pencil line with a finger of my other hand. This is what emerged. I could even feel the beat of his rhythmic steps.*

## HOMEWARD BOUND

### By V. June Collins

Yes, sun nudged, made me notice
That in rays we might melt.
A ridin' along real steady
My hat pulled down of felt.

Could feel sweat band on hat.
Wind sifting through my sleeve.
The passing ground a shrinkin',
As his strides reached into eve.

He so smoothly drifts along,
In his swinging gaited walk.
Communion felt between us,
Left no need to speak or talk.

Mind's on reaching home base
And of chow 'n bed 'n such.
Would end another weary day,
Near feel its soft caring touch.

Old saddle still a squeakin'
In its steady rythmns beat.
Shadows soon start coolin'.
Glad to leave today's heat.

Another day turns to evening,
Daylight vanishes into dark.
Lights occasionally speaking
From hoof beats' fiery spark.

We topped that final distance
On trail leading down to ranch.
Along the creek that tumbled
O'er boulders of its branch.

Been ridin' for the home place
On my horse's radar beam.
In confidence, astraddle
Of a ground-covering machine.

Sure bent on eating distance
In his determined aggressive way.
Corral gate loomed out of shadows,
He's more than earned our pay.

Photo By V. June Collins

"Tracks," feeling a bit embarrassed after getting his spring hair cut. The next day you would have thought it was all his idea, in getting rid of all that shaggy long hair.

Photo By V. June Collins

White etching of age shows in Track's faithful face.

# TRACKS
## (My old Dog)

### By V. June Collins

Now deer season is finally over.
Seems didn't sow enough to reap.
Wrestled hard and long to get one
But now it's almost a relief.

Patted old rifle with loving care,
Set it back up in its cage.
Cast my eyes upon still another
This one's size, is gauge.

Been sitting in the background
So quiet, could not be heard.
In the gun case, that old shot gun,
Resting and saying not a word.

Air has changed its shirt-sleeves
To an extra warm coat and cap.
For the cool breath of the autumn
Now makes my nostrils crisply snap.

It's nearly bird time in the field.
Didn't receive my word by phones.
That special feel up in the air
Now goes deep inside my bones.

My old dog knows it too, you bet.
It is again that time of year.
Expect he heard the thrashing 'round
While I was pawing through my gear.

He may have heard a time or two
The loud jang! of old shot gun
As breach was opened up and oiled
Until that battering ram was done.

Now when my duds take on that look,
He's seen me wearin' through years.
A snap to attention, goes my dog
And cocks up both his ears.

Tail wags sideways, back and forth,
Then gayly 'round and 'round.
Putting love into his every bounce,
Nary a foot stays on the ground.

He leaps and hops and bounds about,
Like a loose rock in a can.
Is trying to say, Lets go! Lets go!
I'm ready, I am! I am! I am!

Great feelings of joy when time to go
Now is shared by both me and thee.
It's a special right bestowed alone
Between my dog, my gun, and me.

Tracks worked serious through years
Except his first one, considered pup.
I packed canteen also for his thirst,
As gladly watched him slurp it up.

He'd flush deer from the thickets,
Put them past me for to see.
Would watch with me, while on stand
With anxious breathing, like statue be.

Pheasant hunts were so very special
Work 'n points before a flush.
One's never really hunted game
Unless used good dog to beat the brush.

My old dog, Tracks, has been a joy.
Now, white shows in his face.
Has spent his life in pleasing me,
So a crown to him I place.

I know that I am a softy, where
My dog, Tracks, is concerned.
But love and happiness are greatest.
It's one thing I have learned.

Small things put a smile upon my lips,
A glow around my heart, to shout,
With a warmth way down inside.
Just who's going to take it out?

They say you can't take it with you
But durned if I won't try.
There's so much joy in this old world,
Sure be hard to go and pass it by.

## HE'S GONE:

*It's not the same without my dog.*
*'Tis sorta flat 'n like a chore.*
*Miss watching my old dog's talents*
*That made my wearies rise 'n soar.*

*Original Painting "Passion," painted during a time in my life, I was attempting to interpret, different type feelings, into my paintings.*

*The Poem "Passion," was written as I was working on the original picture -- 2-23-1962,*

During the time I was working on the original picture, a friend came to visit one evening. He asked, "What do you think you are doing?" I replied --"Well, what does it look like to you? He gave a arrumph! sorta sound, and hesitated a second or so, and replied, "It look like two love sick "Polley Wogs" to me." I laughed aloud! Yes, success unexpected, no less.

## PASSION

By V. June Collins

Signals emote, leap space, distance a room
Throbbing ignites, our beings into tune.

A Magnetic attraction, direct, melting through aims,
To current exciting, that courses our veins

A smile, a glance smolders, a touch of a hand,
Your firing loves embers, to glowing my man

Together us drawing, for to be not controlled,
As if forever wanting me, in your arms to hold.

Floating and drifting, orbiting in space,
Engulfed and entwined into possessive embrace

With need so completely, is fanned into flame;
Desire kindling and ashes, consumed without shame.

Pressing, demanding, keen passion bursts of its bonds,
Leaving endearing contentment, as if touched by a wand.

# BRONZE DAUNSAY (DANCER)
## (1962)
### By V. June Collins

I have waited, not patiently,
For Tango's colt to be born.
But then he arrived suddenly,
During a loud thunder storm.
    Was both surprised and happy
    To receive the glad word,
      So spurred old jeep, onward
      Up the road like a bird.
Far up in corner of deer pasture,
Where both of them stood,
Tango nickered, serenely
As only a proud mother would.
    Bronze, tall and wobbley,
    Stubbed along at her side,
    Wishing he could find
    Some quiet place for to hide.
We worked and we coaxed him
Just to suck the right place.
Could not keep his interest
Past drizzle of milk on his face.
    But toil as he would,
    Real often, then rest,
    Dinner still evaded him,
    While trying his best.
David and I soon decided
To take them off to the barn.
Where the weather and wind
Could do them no harm.
    Weaving unsurely about,
    He truckled along.
    While Tango continued
    To sing him her song.

But food he must have,
I was soon to decide.
So four bottles full
He was forced to imbibe.
    Quite a bit on his face
    And some spilled all around,
    Getting about three bottles inside,
    Rest on the ground.
By morning his appetite
Had so much increased
His trouble was nil.
Tits popped in, as if greased.
    He smacked and he guzzled
    And his tail did a spin,
    As the milk gurgled down
    To his belly within.
For a couple of days,
When bucking he'd try,
He'd jump up and down
In one place and sigh.
    The third day he felt
    Like a man and must show
    How hard he could kick
    And the length of the blow.
By fourth he'd let go whizzers,
At least little chance.
I swatted him proper
With a wham to the pants.
    The fifth day in the barn lot,
    He raced with a spurt.
    Tango went chasing him
    For fear he'd get hurt.
Around, back and forth,
His speed such a thrill.
With mud all on the ground,
He's surely to spill.

He slammed on his brakes,
Too late he soon found.
Bounced off of woven wire fence
And back on the ground.
    He picked himself up,
    Covered muddy, pretty bad
    His mom was quite ruffled
    And a little bit mad.
She had been trying to tell him
He'd fall on his face.
That mud in the barn lot
Was not a place for a race.
    But, like most little boys,
    What did a mom really know.
    He dashed back again
    To make a much bigger show.
Right up to the back fence.
He stopped with a chounce,
Wheeled back, as a show off,
Ended up in a bounce.
    When out flew his feet
    In all directions at once,
    Landed all skittled up,
    Feeling the looks of a dunce.
For the rest of the day
He was as good as could be,
He ate, slept and dreamed
So his Tango would see.
    Sunday morning, his 6th day,
    Again sun began to shine
    So I turned them to pasture
    With hope they'd be fine.
He romped and he played.
At *barbwire fence stops quick.
But the third time and pass
The old wire took its nick.

***Barbed-wire:** Correct perhaps. We call it barb-wire.

He couldn't stop soon enough,
He tumbled on through.
The wire slashed away
And the blood shone through.
    He scrambled and thrashed
    With fright to get up.
    Friends tried to help him.
    In their arms circled to cup.
He squeezed away in alarm
Toward mom in fast return.
Dashed back among searing wire
With its rip slashing burn.
    Barbs scratched and grab.
    With each move it hurt.
    Ripped his tender skin open
    With every lunge, more curt.
Back into straw covered stall,
Doc started stitching him back.
For a time he'd be grounded
In this square, padded shack.
    Stayed with he and his mom
    Both days and five nights
    Being sure our Bronze darling
    Was kept mending all right.
His wounds soon could heal,
Nearly as good as if new
And again, be turned out
'Neath sky, waiting so blue.
    Like his mom, we love him,
    Truly, Yes! Very much!
    More loving kindness felt
    In each loving touch.

(ca-1980's) Photographer unknown

**The Martin Crew Cowboys returning from cattle drive over Sheep Rock to Grass Lake. They are: Lindsay Martin on Squanto; Virgil Houdeshell on Tootia Bug; Brice Martin on Gus: Rance Martin on Rio; J. T. Martin on Sugar Pine; Pat Martin on Strawberry; Wes Jones on Nuggett; Robyn Jones on-; Robert Martin on Dolly.**

According to Brice Martin, a 4th generation pioneer, his uncle Jesse Martin told him that their ancestors the Haight brothers, Charles and Cornelius, built the cattle trail over Sheep Rock in the 1880's. The Haight brothers used a one horse or oxen plow, around the north end of Sheep Rock, for carving the trail. The trail was used as a cattle trail to drive Haight's cattle from Little Shasta to Butte and Antelope Creeks. The Martins have continued using the same trail to move cattle from Table Rock Ranch in Little Shasta to Grass lake in the spring, and back to Table Rock each fall, still as of October 15, 2003. The Coonrod Ranch in the 1920's also, began using the old Sheep Rock trail. *(Information from: Pat & Brice **Martin**)*

Photo By V. June Collins

**Sheep Rock,** was an obstacle that had to be reckoned with, when pioneers reached Shasta Valley, with its hard and difficult decent to valley floor. However, they were able to recuperate and, rest for a time at Barnum Springs, located near the southern base of Sheep Rock, after their long arduous journey.

# SUNSET ON SHEEP ROCK
### By V. June Collins

Sheep Rock stands strong,
Determined, winds blowing loud.
While watching over the valley
Is so mighty and proud.

Herds under rim are lowing,
Restless and long.
Mothers are calf calling
with their cow-balling song.

Quiet still starts descending,
Contentments overtake.
Full bellies start resting
In huddles they make.

The dust from their hooves
In shadows fade out.
The coyotes and creatures
Start slinking about.

While cloak of the evening
Seems to hover in cold,
The paint left from sunshine
Glows strawberry-gold.

Another day, so worth living,
For that few minutes' view.
This sunset is here etched
In my memories anew.

*Poem page 74 was written by me in tribute to Doc, February 7, 1963. Doctor Albert Newton was our doctor for many years. He was also the only doctor left in our comunity during WWII. He would often be seen going to and from the hospital or a residence at any hour of the day or night and many extra hours in behalf of people in this community. We often wondered how he endured the lack of sleep. Yes, he did make house calls, willingly.*

*Doc was the Drill Captain of the Sheriff Posse's Drill Team for a number of years. All riders were dressed in Union, Civil War uniforms, with authentic eagle and crest, brass buttons adorning each, which Doc had acquired for all the uniforms, plus authentic sabers, saddles and gear. My husband Jerry, was one of this unit, was also its secretary for a number of years. Jerry as well as some other riders, owned their own saddles and gear.*

*In the July 4th, Centennial Parade, held in Reno, Nevada in 1964, The Siskiyou Sherriff's Posse competed against the Sacramento's Sheriff Posse's, Top Palamino, drill team, and took first place, returning home to Yreka with a very large 5' high, "Sweepstakes," over all Trophy. Later it was stolen from out of the Posse Hall, and never retrieved.*

*Doc's birthday always comes to mind, on May 31st, his and Charlie Cooley's birthday being the same day as mine- only different years.*

Photo By V. June Collins

## " DOC "
### (Albert H. Newton)

### By V. June Collins

From each of us, this you'll see
And a surge of gratitude from me.
Doc's not so tall and slightly grey,
Quick and brusk and on his way.
Calls come in all times by the hour,
Enough to make most folks glower.
But not this man our towns so proud
And here can say it clear and loud.
We're mighty lucky this town he chose
To fix its bruises and wipe its nose.
Another thing that I'd like to mention
The Posse boys he calls to attention.
An accomplishment of no small size
As over the hill they fall and rise.
Columns right and then four abreast
Single file and columns left.
His black steed canters along the line
With Doc as stiff as starch and fine.
Black flowing plume swoops from his hat.
Now fall in line - don't stop to chat.
Work and drill, that's what they need
On wobbly horses and gallant steed.
Some look fine when whipped in shape
But damn - if some a soldier make.
If Sarg. Bryan would chew off some tails,
Kick behinds and boot the snails.
You'd have it made, a group so sharp
So closely knit, can't pry apart.
But then it seems a job so done
Might just be finished before begun.

Photo By Jerry Collins

Top: Fence standers Candy Brewer, her mom, Artise (Murray) Brewer and Candy's brother, Jess "Cappy" Brewer.

Jess and Artise chose Jerry & I as Godparents for Candy and Cappy when they were just young sprouts.

We had all gone up to the corral to look over a gelding brought in from Idaho, before deciding to make a purchase of him for Candy.

This ranch was then situated on the property, where Fairchild Medical Center is built today.

*In 1962, A Buckskin called "Nattie" was a gift to Candy Brewer when a youngster, (we were her Godparents) They were living on Dorothy Hill's place, where Yreka Junction is today. Conversation between she and the horse follows.*

## CANDY AND NATURAL SWEET

By V. June Collins

You came up to my pasture
in hope, wishing to see,
A horse, you kept praying
would your very own be.

I gave you that look
and up hoisted, tail high.
Put an arch in my neck
and went sailing right by.

I stopped to show you,
with a few bites of hay,
that my appetite's good
without further delay.

While my prancing around
is to dispel all your doubt,
at my age... I might be...
an old plod, or a lout.

I wasn't born yesterday.
So I'm not a spring chicken.
Thought of games, I laugh.
My pulse seemed to quicken.

With my head lifted high
I then sniffed in the breeze.
While Jerry and Wally seemed
to played tag in the trees.

That coy bit of oats offered
is really old shoe.
Will you just try again,
with something else new?

I knew they'd soon give up
So I pranced down the lane.
I was gallantly pretending wild,
high-stepping and vain.

When I see the jig, was up,
As shut slammed the gate.
What ever should I do...but
Just stand there, and wait?

I know one thing for sure,
Now, I must act my best.
For surely, this will be,
The most important test.

Candy, if you could have me
and give me a home.
I would be, never again,
Just left out, all alone.

I can feel you softly, praying
as you're stroking my nose.
I hear, "you'd love me forever,
from my head to my toes."

I closed my eyes slightly,
While I listened and knew.
Sound of Candy's thoughts...
Peacefully, coming on through.

Nattie's long shaggy coat,
I know, kept him warm.
Out east of the our State
in its icy cold storm.

Now, I'll curry and comb.
My loving care will flow.
Yes, his color I do like...
Can most see and I know.

See the shimmering shine, his
summers sleek tights, will take.
Each strand softly, dusted,
in golds, fresh dewy flake.

Nattie, I so plainly see you,
My breath taken away.
I gasp... from your beauty.
Your visions, here to stay.

Listen!
Could that be my name?
The best ever, I'm graced.
"Natural Sweet," like a crown,
on top of head, you've placed.

Then I hear "Nattie," again,
like a song, on your voice.
Candy! My radiant master!
You're gladly, my choice.

Please, take me to your pasture,
just about, any time soon.
I'm yours, and all paid for...
from Jerry and June.

Jess Brewer on Bogie.                                      Photo By V. June Collins

Jess and his family were next door neighbors of ours in the 1950's /1960's. We, at that time, all lived on Oregon street near the Court House. Jess and his wife Ardice (Murray) Brewer were both good friends.

We enjoyed many activities with them, including painting, hunting, fishing and horse oriented, Sheriff Posse search and rescue with its Civil War parade group. Jess was the Siskiyou County probation officer a number of years in Yreka. At the early age of 39 years Jess was taken from us by a heart attack.

# RAMROD BREWER

By V. June Collins

In Saturday's special, a shirt made of plaid,
Dad gummedest, wearin'est one that you had,
Your blustery arrival for coffee and chat
Brought a shimmer of joy where ever you sat.

Your boisterous laughter warmed each our souls
With your love of life, dogs, horses and foals.
We know now, however long that we live,
You had a charm, a warmth, to freely give.

Our life is much richer, inspired by your will.
Especially when memories become quiet and still.
Your enthusiasm swelled like the rise of a river,
Joined together our hunts, as bow, arrow and quiver

Your vibrating echoes moved us all into gear.
To a new task we'd be off, loudly to cheer.
Fired to painting, you pumped full our vein
'Til our hands reached to master images plain.

Times we'd be resting, perhaps in the shade.
You'd mention boats, a cabin, a chess board of jade.
We'd perk up our ears and roll up a sleeve.
Tear into a job, with a toss and a heave.

I've seen you smile, as we're most moving an ocean.
So pleased with yourself in midst of commotion.
As we're happily lugging your will into view.
Huck Finn, so it seems, had nothing on you.

Always a come back, your eyes give a spark.
Your gay quips, a joke, a tidbit, a lark.
If things became slow, bitching you'd start.
'Til finally I'd flare and fly all apart.

You'd guffaw a laugh, 'twould frighten the breeze.
For all the time waiting the results of your tease.
With a big raise from June would complete be your day.
Sure, you would just smile, swagger and saunter away.

Photo By Jerry Collins

Jess Brewer fence sitting with daughter Candice Brewer.

"Candy," Candice Brewer and her parents Artise (Murray) Brewer; Jess Brewer and her brother, "Cappie" Jess Brewer. Panning for gold at our mine up Nordheimer Creek.

Photo By V. June Collins

Photo By Jerry Collins

Dean and Candy (Brewer) Mott visiting with V. June Collins at the 1997 Fathers Day, Annual CHVA ( Classic Vehicles Association) car show, held at Siskiyou Golden fair grounds in Yreka, California. Many car clubs come for the days festivities.

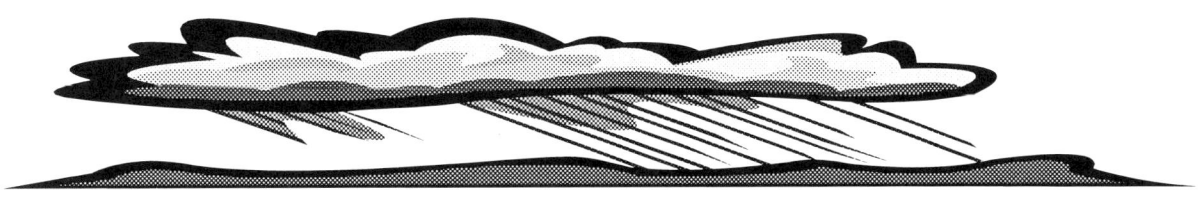

### CULTIVATING HE GOES
By V. June Collins

OUR PASTURE NEEDED TURNING.
Equipment, just didn't own.
Talked of time to work it
Before springs sunshine's shone.

JERRY TRAVELED TO THE FEED STORE.
Saw sign of "Witch for Sale".
Loaded up that man eater, as
said, "Could rent before a sale."

HE WORKED FURROWS SIDE BY SIDE.
Had 'em lookin' pretty straight.
Some of time was going good
Others were grunt, groan 'n fate.

PUSHED 'N DRUG HIM AGAINST HIS WILL.
A snortin' with deliberate strength.
He'd end up wrestling it each time,
As he made that turn from length.

THE SKY BEGAN TO LOOSE ITS BLUE.
Clouds started nudging over head.
He still had quite a bit to finish
So sighed, to revive his lead.

HE HEARD A DISTANT ROLL OF THUNDER.
Knew he shouldn't be out in field.
Then said to self, "Will finish
this row, before I stop 'n yield."

TO BE IN FIELD WITH METAL MONSTER,
With lightning so close about.
Sure not smart, he'd understood,
While closer, it began to shout.

HE STAGGERED TO THE VERY END.
Turned 'n backed her in disgust.
To make that next row line up
She was sure no living trust.

HE MUST HAVE WAITED A BIT TOO LONG.
Felt lightning strike its blow.
It rattled his every timber
And shook him both to and fro.

THOUGHT HE SURELY MUST BE DEAD!
That lightning had struck him down.
The rain was pounding in his ears
And splattering on the ground.

FOR AS HE'D BACKED 'N JERKED HER
To make that next row hence...
Felt wild chattering between his ears
HE'D JUST BACKED INTO ELECTRIC FENCE!

This sign hung on the side of our house for many years,
And gradually became Buckskin Acres.

# THE CALL OF THE WIND

(Summer's Breath)

By V. June Collins

**"Its dust devils and whirl-winds"**

The Indian's soul is at unrest today
Was told by the wind as stopped to play.
It's a lonely sound when first you hear
The wailing sighs, like man in fear.

It soon makes you feel so all alone
As prairies filled with sun bleached bone.
Alto voices from the screen porch I heard
Was soprano wails, on wires, in word.

Bass low moans in the barn loft high
As the wind rushed on toward the sky.
It gathers souls at this time of year,
To again, oversee their land so dear.

With soft moccasin'd feet and silver bow,
They ride high on wind, make friend of foe.
See now 'n then, a moccasin toe touch ground.
At least the dust, no tracks, I've found.

ART WORK: *By V.June Collins.*

For a gusty breeze when going so fast,
Imprints are at once sucked up in blast.
Summer times you'll see a renegade now and then,
That kicks up some dust in his haste to ascend.

      The dust spirals and glides across over the plain,
      Scatters good earth to ancestors, forever to reign.
      The breeze of the west, blows cold on their bones,
      That once were as warm as the sun on the stones.

           When I hear wind whistling its wild little tune,
           I smile, think gladly, come back again soon.
           For here's to the wind's loud carol disguise,
           Playing choruses over to old and the wi

Making souls happy, is such a fine thing to win,
      I'll know when I hear you, you're together again.

*Written 1/12/1965 during the 64-65 flood. It rained for days without let-up. It snowed, then rained some more, forcing the waters much higher than the 1880 flood (marked on a tree in Orleans, California) or the 1955 floods by far. The devastation along the Klamath and Salmon Rivers and their tributaries was incomprehensible or unimaginable without having seen the total destruction and felt its wrath. In some places it was one hundred and fifty feet higher than the regular high water line. Most everything slicked and gone. Some strangely, left deposited, in another area.*

## HUNGRY WATER

### By V. June Collins

Warm was the rain that dispelled all doubts
Of the liquid snow from upon the mounts.
That soon would flow with mighty wrath
Around the doors and village path.

A sullen rain, steady, still and wet
Running quietly by between lull and fret.
Catching its breath, returned again strong.
Kept marching days, through nights so long.

Angry rain with wind tossing head,
Jerking about as wild colts when led.
Pawing and crashing around in fear,
Fighting and kicking at trees when near.

Determined rain, would it ever stop?
As it spread like mercury with every drop.
Struggling and coughing for lower ground
'Til soon none was left to be found.

First the wild water came dashing in fright,
To get far away quickly with all of it might.
As deeper it got, seemed to half change its mind,
Some still wanted to go and some stay behind.

Clinging wildly to objects laying close in path
While roiling in agony as torn with its wrath.
Clutching at trees and what ever it found.
Confused, wicked water was stealing up ground.

It grabbed at the bridges as if to hang on,
With weight and burden, soon they too were gone.
In desperation was grasping for all in its reach,
Sucking down tightly, as the mouth of a leech.

Clutched in death's struggle, tons writhing past,
While mixed logs and debris were piling up fast.
Logs crazed with desire to ride higher the crest
Would dive up from bottom, tumble over for rest.

Then with excitement of a stampeding mob
Crashed onward power to a grinding sob.
Roaring in anguish and clawing for air,
Boiling up boulders with fits of despair.

With noise and confusion clamped tightly in jaws,
Forcing forward a path, without any pause.
Pushing and crowding with weight from above.
Overseeing an opening with a poke and a shove.

Angered, it's fearsome, to the mild and the strong,
Making each of us little in singles and throng.
Can just snuff us out, no trouble, with ease,
At most any moment, whenever it please.

We're insignificant, so tiny and weak,
Even us loud mouths, preferably meek.
Has left life bedraggled, both weary and lost.
A high toll of recovery, things missing and cost.

It's true she wiped clean just many a spot
But left the crevasse with the wedging it got.
Replenished old bedrock, by a river well done.
A wealth of new gold to gleam in the sun.

With help from each other bound to come through
These forever neighbors are a pretty close crew.
It's grab up your boot straps and give each a tug
And a swat to the back of each adjoining lug.

Lives that were spared are so dear to this part
While beginning anew is still from the heart.
These waters are pure and air feels so clean,
It's the best place to live ever I've seen.

Good waters so precious to each of us all,
For pastures, for drinking, in glasses so tall.
Now we're to live a life such as He wills
In solitude on the Salmon, in peace on the hills.

*This poem "HUNGRY WATERS" was previously published, By **Melvina Boynton** of Orleans, California. and Printed by Nolan Lithio of Yreka, California. In her book, **"The 1964 FLOOD DISASTER,"** showing her many pictures of devastation, along the Klamath River. During its struggle to survive, and the aftermath, as left around places of Orleans,*

Photos By V. June Collins

High water during this 1964/65 flood cleaned the banks high above where the bridge once crossed, also stole its bridge, 8 miles below The Forks of Salmon, California. The cable shown in place from the Nordheimer, down river, abutment side, in order to receive supplies to their side of the river. This cable was used for some time until a temporary structure was in place. Later another bridge was built.

A short time after receiving a call via ham radio, (phone lines all out) as to what was needed in line of repairs from the flood damage area where Leo and Rose Brown lived on Nordheimer Creek, Jerry and June Collins hauled a pickup load including this roll of plastic pipe over to the Browns. Leo, with help, then pulled these across in relay loads to their side of the river on this cable. After reloading into their vehicles, they took them home. For both temporary and permanent repairs to water lines, destroyed during flood, could then be made.

## JACKET RETREAT

By V. June Collins

So, old Jean Jacket,
Yah had a busy season.
Now slow up, whoa!
Listen to reason.

These cold winter days
I'm just plain cold.
A change is overdue,
On this I'm told.

You're shunted aside
By a Mackinaw warm.
For braving chills
Of a coming storm.

When spring again
Lifts its gay old head,
You'll be bounced out
Of a warm winter bed.

Yes, I mistook your sigh
 For deep despair,
As those lazy snowflakes
Softly, filled the air.

But I was wrong,
As I chanced another look.
Oh! such a lively old jacket,
Hung up, on a hook.

Photo By V. June Collins

Gladly clinging...
To that nail on wall.
While desperately trying
So not, to fall.

Draped with others
Behind kitchen door.
Closely spaced
Above boots on floor.

Slumped are your shoulders,
Elbows together.
You look so satisfied
Out of the weather.

All through the nights
Of winter long.
A hanging in shadows
Of Christmas song.

The glowing fireplace
Reflects in lights.
On battered symbol
Of hard working sights.

Slowly, drowsy waves
Of sleep descends.
On your each worn seam
With need of mends.

Your stretching yawn...
Wrapped in deep content.
With warmth and joy
Being most heaven sent.

Christmas Eve lingers
In morning's long wait.
You're a comfort, old friend,
With memories great.

A rustle of footsteps,
Lights, a tree.
With a gasp of delight,
Here, for all to see.

Gifts abound...
While sheer pleasures flow,
See the looks youngsters'
Up-turned faces show.

Still darkness fading
Into dawn of new day.
Another Merry Christmas
In every which way.

# SNOW CAME AGAIN IN APRIL

By V. June Collins

Snow flakes afloat in swirling draft
Come down among trees, fore and aft.
All adrift as they plan to stay.
Unattached they glide away.
I gaze above into a whirling mass,
Separate shapes, all downward cast.
By the closest breeze and wispy wind
They flutter up and again descend.
Soundproofing tracks with fluffy mist,
In turns and spirals do the twist.
Peace seems nestled high on a ledge,
Crystals shimmer from each tiny edge.
Piles of snowflakes in grand array,
When the sun comes out to melt away.
Glistened, twinkled in shivering fright,
What the sun would do with all its might.
Alas, was saved by Blanket, the cloud,
When he hovered close and said aloud,
"Never fear, I'm here to cover...
Jolly Old Sun, today, I'll smother.
I'll bring more snowflakes again tonight.
They'll arrive in fury on midnight flight.
I'll cover you deep so Sun can't see,
And freeze a crust, reserved for thee
To hold your classic fingers of dew
That moistens slowly for all to view."
Spring has hidden charms, a chest of jewels,
Grass, bulbs, flowers. Ah! nature's tools.
Sleep my snowflakes, close your eyes,
No need to worry about the changing skies.
So drift way deep, by the old front door.
We will need you again, as always before.

## SPRINGS RESTLESS SUNSHINE

By V. June Collins

The SUN came out and frisked about
with gay shadows of the CLOUD.
Their plump, gracious, frothy forms
grew thin while crying loud.

Said, "You're forever chasing us,
o'er mountain tops so high.
We're trying hard to gather up
to have another cry."

But wafted away on air-foam pads,
out of sight and mind,
Old "SOL," at last alone was left,
to a playmate elsewhere find.

The SUN came out, glared real hard
at the black loam in the field.
First she stood, returned his stare,
tried hard not to yield.

His gaze became too much to stand,
seems SOIL sort of bowed her head.
If SPRING is bound to come
she would start warming up her bed.

Steam, softly started in to rise
in curls. It wisped about.
The SEEDS began to snuggle down
for growing roots so stout.

Stretching toes and raising arms
made room for bodies strong.
Then, right before my very eyes,
They're seen growing right along.

Hands reached up into the air,
waved happily in the breeze.
They wrinkled up their noses,
laughed, pollen made them sneeze.

Time came to dry their tears of joy
that linger on the tips.
They nodded heads, kissed the dew,
from one another's lips.

For soon again, new mown hay
smelled good upon the air.
SUN shined hot, again, beating down,
in its drying-kind of stare.

Grasses drying, soon loaded in
the old ram-shackled barn.
'Tis the way SUN doth shine
down here, upon the farm.

Photo By Jerry Collins

We rode a mile from our camp at Campbell Lake, upto the blue waters of Cliff Lake. Some of us fished a bit, and others lolled around in the shade. On our return back to camp, we brought back a burro load of snow from a snow bank, for ice box purposes. Those circled for the photo are Greg Collins behind his dad, Lael Collins on Tango; Jo Blevins Butler on Topaz; Carolyn Collins on Blue; Ernie Lemos; V. June Collins on Whisper; Agnes lemos on Boots; June Severns on Rocky; and Keith Severns on Blackie.

*Those involved in the following Poem were friends and family, June & Keith Severns; Ernie & Agnes Lemos; Our son & wife, Lael & Carolyn Collins & grandson, Greg Collins; My Mother, Jo Blevins, Butler; My husband, Jerry Collins; & myself.*

### BEATING THE HEAT

( A July 1967 happening)

By V. June Collins

4TH OF JULY CAME SIDLING UP.
We friends began to bunch.
JERRY and I saddled up horses,
as on last of hay they munch

KEITH, JUNE, ERNIE, AND AGNES
Hove in among the dust.
Slammed shut the tail gate.
Yelled Powder River or bust!"

CAROLYN, LAEL, AND GRANDMA JO.
We're all headin" for the hills.
Back into The Marbles once again,
to absorb solitude that fills.

MADE OUR CAMP AT CAMPBELL LAKE.
Later on, had lunch in afternoon.
Then someone said, "I need ice!
To make this here drink bloom."

Another voice chimed in quick,
"At LAKE CLIFF, there's yet snow."
So put pack saddle on DICKEY MULE.
Soon, short mile up mountain go.

TIED UP HORSES, SOME FISHED A BIT,
others rested, lolled around in shade...
'til evening shadow started sinking
and the sunshine began to fade.

THEN LED LITTLE MULE TO SNOWBANK.
Shoveled in snow to each side,
when suddenly, he came un-glued.
'Twas most freezing of his hide.

HE BUCKED, JUMPED, 'n BRAYED.
The *ALFORKUSES bounded high.
Hoof prints covered snowbank,
while snowballs filled the sky.

OF COURSE, NOTHING YET SECURED.
He soon unloaded all that cold.
Stood spraddle legged 'n defiant,
Still insulted 'n quite bold.

**\*Alforjas,** *Is of Spanish Origin, pronounced AL FORE HASS, (pack bags or panniers that hang on packhorse saddle).* **\*ALFORKUS**,*is a corrupted English pronunciation used by many old timers, including my parents, grandparents and myself.*

FINALLY LOADED SNOW AGAIN
and back down trail did wind.
Got supper started on the fire.
COLD SCREWDRIVERS tasted fine.

WE IN COMPLETE CONTENTMENT SAT,
some on logs and ground,
before all hell broke loose
from the quiet all around.

Camp neighbor, DICK McCURDY,
Came ridin' toward the lake with zest.
He rode straight for the waters edge
as sun was sinking in the west.

WE THOUGHT HE'D WATER HIS HORSES.
Instead, he hazed them in with lunge.
They obeyed his very loud commands.
Even horses lead, made the plunge.

ON OUT A-PAST A DROP OFF POINT
they all, disappeared from sight.
We sat there in dumfoundment,
watched as vanished, without a fight.

WE GASPED, 'n WAITED AN ETERNITY,
what seemed a day and night.
Now, bubbles only, were surfacing.
Finally, a hat popped into sight.

WILD WATER BROKE, BOILED AGAIN.
As thrashing feet and heads appear.
We jumped to our feet, in unison...
With all gladness, gave a cheer.

ALL SPLASHING WILDLY, DRIPPED ASHORE.
Tragedy, by luck, was spared.
While the void left in our guts
Was totally, among us shared.

THIS FOOLISH STUNT COULD HAVE RUINED
All of our vacation, in these hills.
Made a shudder run through ranks.
Was a sobering thought, that chills.

WE ATE OUR SUPPER BY LANTERN LIGHT.
Sure we're glad to be alive, 'n well.
Soon, crawled down into sleeping bags
As fitfully, all sleeping fell.
THIS
SECOND PART
(Was written in March 1993)
AFTER RE-READING POEM
(of then 26 years ago)
AS I WAS TO BE GIVING POEM
AT YREKA 'S COMMUNITY THEATER,
THIS APRIL NIGHT,

....
- INTRODUCTION -
TONIGHT IT IS..MY PRIVILEGE
TO AGAIN, BE SHARING MY POETRY
WITH YOU FOR THE 4th YEAR.
....
ANOTHER HIGHLIGHT TONIGHT
(IS HAVING MY)
G. GRANDDAUGHTER - TRACY COLLINS
OF SUSANVILLE, CA.
TO HAVE CHOSEN---TO CELEBRATE HER
(10TH BIRTHDAY)
THE FIRST DECADE OF HER LIFE TIME
ATTENDING TONIGHT'S...
COWBOY POETRY & MUSIC SHOW

# MY AFTER THOUGHTS
## (1993)

AFTER THOUGHTS of past to present
Are passing my eyes, in fond review.
Plainly etched, like stone engraved,
Decades add up, to quite a few.

Thoughts formed solid into shapes
for some of these, I now find...
Have differences of mind, in years,
SO NEED TO TURN BACK CLOCK 'n WIND.

GRANDMA JO, had turned seventy four.
A MIRACLE, to my fifties mind.
She hadn't been astride a horse
since some twenty years behind.

My young 'n agile thoughts then
were just a bit out of plumb.
Find, now I've reached familiar hill,
WAS A THINKIN' SORTA DUMB.

It was no miracle at all!
MY MOM, had lots of grit.
She and TOPAZ rode like one.
CAME IN LOOKIN' FINE 'n FIT.

She was raised in saddle too.
In those days, were her wheels.
She climbed aboard, still spry,
adjusted stirrups to the feels.

I'm not nearly in the same shape
My mom was, that special trip.
I have to squat 'n reach 'n grunt
from a hillside boost 'n grip.

My wobbly rise into the stirrup
is indeed a sight that's sad.
My joints creak, knees won't
bend. Down right makes me mad.

My saddle mare, Pink, also aging,
walks slower while others run.
Enjoying life out in pasture,
is still my LITTLE, OLD RED DUN.

To open up youths gates again,
A surprised be. TOO BIG A SHOCK!
Yes, we both enjoyed our ages...but sometimes,
ARE  SECURED BEHIND A LOCK.

# POETRY'S ASSUMED NAMES

By V. June Collins

| | |
|---|---|
| Habit forming poetry | ADICTRY |
| Boring, dull poetry is | BOETRY |
| Co/Authored should be | COETRY |
| Lean, Disconnected verse | DIETRY |
| Money making, poetry | DOETRY |
| Foe, feuding fighting kind | FOETRY |
| Meaningful real free verse | FRETRY |
| Great, good stuff, might be | GOETRY |
| Humorous, amusing stuff | HUMETRY |
| Christmas jingles must be | HO-HOETRY |
| Dumb, ignorant ramblings | IGETRY |
| Jolly, joyful, jingles with sounds of | JOETRY |
| Lifeless, low going nowhere poetry | LOETRY |
| Mediocre, mumbling poetry | MOETRY |
| Returned, refused poetry would be | NOETRY |
| Debt ridden, soon becomes | OWETRY |
| Boatman's chant poetry called | ROETRY |
| Fertile, soddy, earthy poetry | SOETRY |
| Sad, sorrowful poetry is | WOETRY |
| Cowboy, traditional poetry | YEE-HAAETRY |

HAVING FUN MAKING SENSE!

\* Previously Published: 1995 Nov/Dec National Writers Association Magazine & Jan/ 2003. Siskiyou Writer's Plume

Jerry Collins with Sulphur Sannrush "Sann," 1966 Yearling filly, First place winner, Owned by Jerry and V. June Collins, at Second Annual Buckskin Horse Show, Yreka, California.
The first Buckskin Horse Show held in the Nation was held at Siskiyou Golden Fair Grounds, Yreka, CA in 1965, and actively continued annually, here, for twenty-five years.

Photo by V. June Collins

*Poem written 1966. "To Sulphur Sannrush," A Buckskin filly, foaled April 14, 1965 by Rushaway, and out of Topaz Sann. During 30 year period of raising Buckskins horses, and day after tomorrow a yearling.*

### SULPHUR SANN RUSH
(A Buckskin Filly)

*By V. June Collins*

She's a dream, an amber Filly,
   her frosting in black.
   Planting hoof prints
   in each scattered track.

   She's bucking and kicking
   at mostly the air.
   Fanning her hooves
   in the face of the mare.

Runs with the wind,
full tilt to the sound.
Beating in echoes
while pounding the ground.

Shaking her head,
her mane flying high,
Flashing her belly
tipped up to the sky.

Bursts of running
with all of her might,
Sailing back quickly
a beauty in flight.

Filling the pasture
with holes in the grass,
Each time she goes dashing,
classy this lass.

Slides to a stop,
clean down on her heels.
Flips back around,
is spinning her wheels.

Sweat breaks through,
wets chest, loin and face.
She's still drumming up
the likes of a race.

Sides are heaving
and pumping in breath,
Energy's steaming,
still lots of it left.

Nostrils spread
in excitement, wild cast,
Whistles a snort
at the end of each blast.

With an arch in her neck
she circles the lot.
Alas, slowing down,
into high a stepping trot.

Cuts in closely,
ducks under the mare's chin,
Bumps into her squarely,
acts awkward again.

Bucks up and down
in a rocking chair glide,
Soon will be stretched out
flat on her side.

A nap 'n a bit more
with her hide in the sun.
She's a darling, a stinker,
Oh! "Son-a-ma-gun!"

*I wrote this poem after spending most of a day and night in the clutches of an angry blizzard coming off of Mt Shasta, in the 1950's. We owned a 4 X 4 Army Carry All, which we also used as our camping rig. It enabled us to get about during deep snows, and steep streets of winter time, in Dunsmuir, California where we lived at that time. Jerry got a call at the Littrell store, where he worked, from the hospital in Weed, saying, "Their Oxygen supply was getting low." Jerry called and asked us, our two sons, Mike and Lael and me to go along, to make the delivery, a distance of about 25 miles.*

*With our sleeping bags always along with us during the winter months and a lunch aboard, we're pretty confident of some comfort if delayed. Our big truck out of Redding loaded with cylinders had made it as far as Dunsmuir, but could not go any farther North. The driver, Hap Winder, however, said he would come along to help Jerry handle tanks in the deep snow. Mike, Lael and I piled into the rig, too, all hurrying in an effort to arrive before the storm settled into its full blast.*

## BLIZZARD BIER

By V. June Collins

Insists being different, worries and blows
From the natural falling of regular snows.
Uneasily wrenching and thrashing around,
Sidewise advancing fast over the ground.

In riotous confusion, refusing to heed,
Momentum driven, gathers up speed.
Winds loud cries fierce, wailing a moan,
Long fingered drifts caress spaces alone.

In erratic flight at ground level soars
Upon porch and down under the door.
As fear clawing fury is whipped into rage
Wild clutching blizzard, bursts out of cage.

Jerks snow rippled cover, back into air.
Strips cold naked earth, leaving her bare.
Hoards of snowflakes in fright blown away
To another someplace,  perhaps not to stay.

Its crack sifting vacuums, steadily fills.
Pressures so mighty, runs over and spills.
Eddies keep building, out of defiant wrath,
Stealing snow depths from a fore, unto aft.

Yet, faster and faster, throttle soon stuck.
Nothing can stop it from running amuck.
Snapping, snarling, lips tightly curled
Acts as if he's mad, at all of the world.

Engulfed, we stagger, in blinding defeat.
Efforts again, arouse, so numb to our feet.
A door flings open from out of the storm,
To a haven of shelter, insides, all so warm.

Looking from within, blizzard appear magic.
Don't go shake hands, he's cunningly tragic.
Deceitful, wicked, on dishonesties thrive...
Shouting in glee, "Death to all things alive."

*This Poem was triggered by Smoke Currie in a happening of April 1969. He, as a young fellow, was out camping, and rode his grandpa Keith Severns' horse, Jake, down to the (crik) to water the horses. In the following poem, I made comparison of his leg in traction and a calf being roped and tied. I have since been asked by those not familiar with the term, for an explanation. So here goes.*

*Calf roping is a timed event, a running calf is roped from horseback. Rider quickly dismounts, runs down the rope while the horse still is holding catch rope tension. From the calf's back side he dumps the calf from its feet to its side, with a flank and neck hold. He then gathers the under front foot and two back feet together. Slipping the loop, from the one end of this small rope,(called a piggin' string, which is carried by roper, either in his mouth or looped in waist band) over these three feet. With this piggin' string he makes three wraps over to the right, if right-handed. On that third wrap, he slides last wrap into a loop, underneath former wrap, (called a hooey). Quickly he then jerks up to tighten the slack, stands away from the calf, and raises both hand in the air, to stop the timer's stop watch.*

Photo By V. June Collins

"Boots Without Broncs, Shoot'n The Bull." During the National Finals at Oklahoma City - 1979--Arron McCombs, Smoke Currie; Jerry Collins; Jim McCombs, and Keith Severns

## ON THE SMOKEY "C"

### By V. June Collins

My story is short and a bit in a hurry.
About a young guy called ol' Smoke Currie.
He rode old Jake down to the Creek.
Watered his belly 'til it sprung a leak.

Galloped on back at break-neck speed
For old Jake's frisky and not off feed.
With gas pedal stuck and grease on brake
They came sailing fast at a fearful rate.

Up against another horse they slammed.
Smoke's leg caught between battering ram.
Something had to give, 'twas Smoke's leg bone.
And it scared all tar out of each one alone.

Was long, slow road back, such a bumpy trip.
Kept hurting much even when biting your lip.
Back to civilization. Would it come pretty soon?
How good to see Grandpa Keith and Grandma June.

Got your leg all snubbed up, tight in traction.
Looks for a while, your gonna be out of action.
Like roped-up calf when his world goes ca-flewy.
You know how he feels with " 3 wraps and a hooey."

Photo By V. June Collins
Smoke Currie 1969, between shows--National Finals Rodeo, Oklahoma City

*Not long ago, I got to thinking of something my mother in-law once said to me. "That our ears and feet never stop growing during a lifetime." Many other thoughts came into focus. From those thoughts this soon arrived.*

## EARLY AND LATE

By V. June Collins

In early years, age is far, far away.
I'll be forever young always, I know.
But life has a way of getting even
When age arrives it starts to grow.

We have to be, at times, darn tough
Right away, I will sorta mention.
It may not bring us to our knees
But sure makes us pay attention.

While still busy climbing life's ladder
Ever so often, find have missed a rung.
Sometimes getting up from that easy chair
Find the spring has up and sprung.

Veins on legs show blue maps of travel
While legs still traverse best resorts.
Find breath arrives in little short pants
Before can make up mind to doff my shorts.

Feet keeps growing until the end of time
Ears too, will grow until they nearly flap.
Have gained two chins, where once was one
Sadly discover, belly most fills the lap.

Finger joints may look large and knobby.
When shoes fit, bunion still wants to hurt.
Gather up some unknown problems, it seems.
Will need new found answers, to convert.

I've been getting up regular, each morn.
Can be looked at, from here, as VERY WELL.
Still considered life to be pretty good
For the shape I'm in, its almost swell.

I laugh and feel it's great to be alive,
Alternative just might be, somewhat grim.
While another day, looks me straight in face
And boldly, dares me, not to smile or grin.

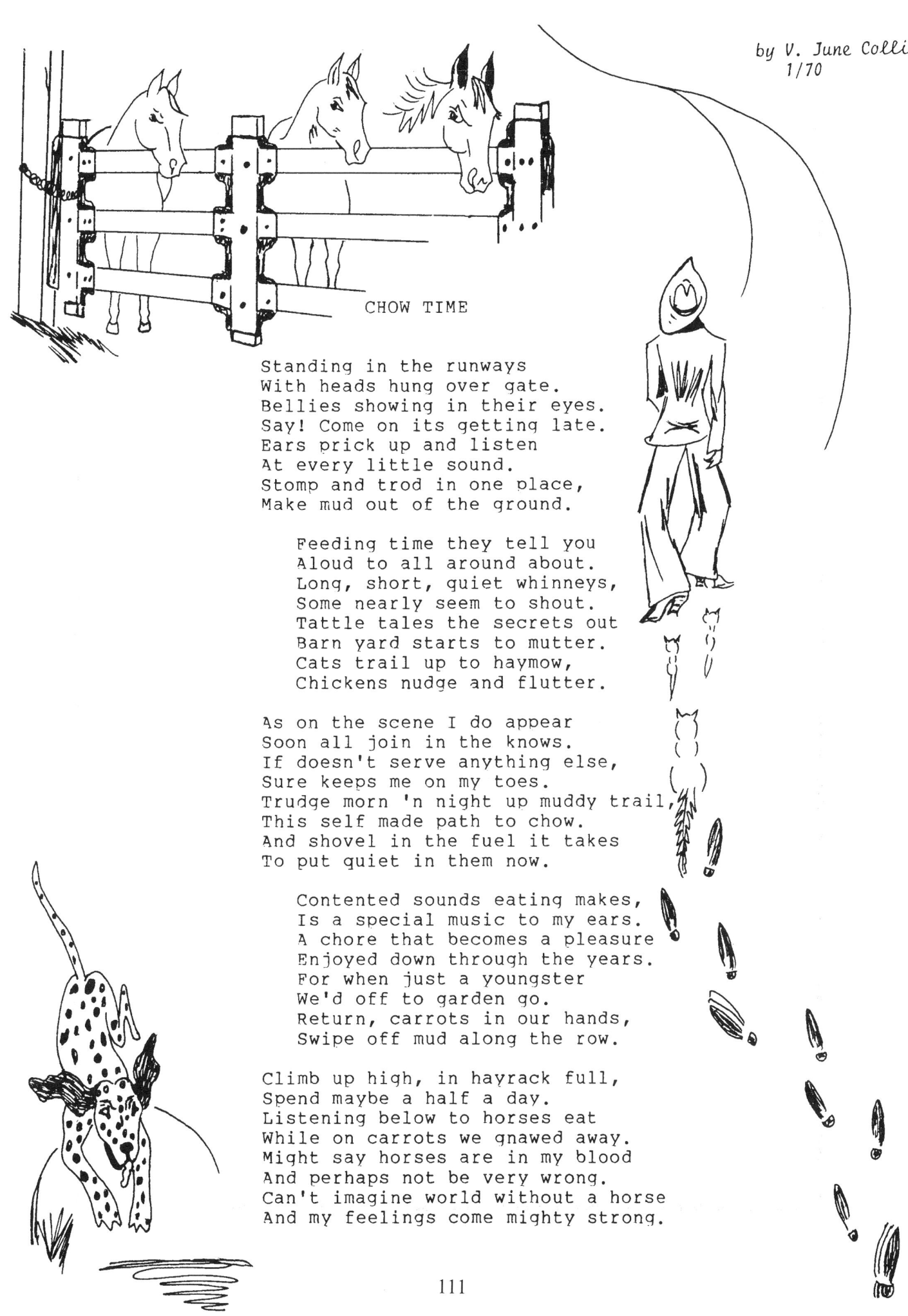

by V. June Collins
1/70

CHOW TIME

Standing in the runways
With heads hung over gate.
Bellies showing in their eyes.
Say! Come on its getting late.
Ears prick up and listen
At every little sound.
Stomp and trod in one place,
Make mud out of the ground.

    Feeding time they tell you
    Aloud to all around about.
    Long, short, quiet whinneys,
    Some nearly seem to shout.
    Tattle tales the secrets out
    Barn yard starts to mutter.
    Cats trail up to haymow,
    Chickens nudge and flutter.

As on the scene I do appear
Soon all join in the knows.
If doesn't serve anything else,
Sure keeps me on my toes.
Trudge morn 'n night up muddy trail,
This self made path to chow.
And shovel in the fuel it takes
To put quiet in them now.

    Contented sounds eating makes,
    Is a special music to my ears.
    A chore that becomes a pleasure
    Enjoyed down through the years.
    For when just a youngster
    We'd off to garden go.
    Return, carrots in our hands,
    Swipe off mud along the row.

Climb up high, in hayrack full,
Spend maybe a half a day.
Listening below to horses eat
While on carrots we gnawed away.
Might say horses are in my blood
And perhaps not be very wrong.
Can't imagine world without a horse
And my feelings come mighty strong.

# POLLEN SPRING POLLEN

By V. June Collins

A sea of white waves before each eye
Until I singled one out against the sky.

In frothy lace, on a branch it hung,
That chosen blossom of the plum.

Soft breath of spring fast at work,
A pollen factory in disguise did lurk.

Everywhere echoes, I hear it callin',
See everywhere, spring and pollen.

Tassels form, hang down with grace,
Dipped in gold. Each fuzzy face.

Drifting pollen shall not miss,
Sends each potion and a kiss.

Spring arms grasp to softly hold.
Pollen paints its touch of gold.

Hummingbirds sip, toasts are a sway.
Bees busily buzz as while away day.

Scattered petals adrift, blossoms fallen.
Pollen in Spring and Spring is Pollen.

Photo By V. June Collins

We have lived in Northern Siskiyou County California and the valley of MT SHASTA all of our married life. The many changing faces and shadows of the mountain, which are ever present, add to its magnetic charm and beauty.

One November 1968 morning, after a light skiff of snow, the outline of giant horse hoof prints on the side of the mountain showed to our elation.

There always seemed to be a need for another picture, as the moods of the mountain are many. This time, after getting the prints back, I was so pleased that I had it enlarged. The following poem also resulted among my many thoughts while studying the picture along with my daughter-in-law, Carolyn Collins. Also the photo shows in the foreground, some of the early construction, in progress, of I-5 Freeway.

*When viewing this photo (enlargement) of Mt Shasta, we found 34 separate images and faces that seem to make the mountain take on a very special feel. I have separately outlined each of these images, onto a page of overlay parchment, for its interest. Yet... This is another story.*

*First came many thoughts of other old legends and slogans. I shall repeat a few to refresh your memories.*

## WE HAVE LEGENDS

By V. June Collins

Minnesota has PAUL BUNYAN
And "Babe," the mighty big blue ox.
They tamed the darkened wilderness
Long before Plymouth Rocks.

Humboldt has their BIG FOOT .
In logging woods he's trod.
Beneath redwoods left his prints
Seen deep down in the sod.
(California)
Now is he a myth the ABOMINABLE
SNOW MAN? Many say not.
Have seen hairy beast rush past,
Left an odorous smell of rot.
(Himalayas)
Here Beans and sugar sweet peas,
Are grown tall and slender.
With acres of asparagus stalks
Grown only tender.

He strides through his fields
Bold, strong and defiant.
"HO! HO! HO!" thunders
THE JOLLY GREEN GIANT!
( from-Blue Lake, Minnesota)

Now we have, "SISKIYOU,"
With his story to tell.
Straight out of history
Yes! To toll like a bell.

*Photos By Jerry Collins*
*Six hard spots, six stones, (rock out-croppings) on the Klamath River that marked the early day trail crossing of the river by the French fur trappers. This was up river a few miles easterly of where the Klamathon bridge is located today.*
*The northeast slope of Black Mountain (note,) is visible in the background.*

### The Legend of
### "S I S K I Y O U"
### &
### Artwork
### By V. June Collins

The meaning of SISKIYOU
has sources three fold.
Some believe 'tis French word,
others Indian I'm told.

The FRENCH translation:
Six hard spots, six stones.
Down on Klamath River,
among fossils and bones.

A FORD, marked for crossing
a giant of streams,
To guide across safely,
on fur trapper dreams.

Then we have another,
that for itself speaks,
On mountain of SISKIYOU,
'n tribal ground treek's. (treks)

*Art work By V. June Collins

Named for a CAYUSE HORSE,
with a stub of a tail,
Which roams this land,
in snow, rain and hail.

In legend, so old!
way back out of past,
A gallopin' so freely,
over our land so fast.

Now most of you have heard,
without any remorse,
THE WANDERING OF SISKIYOU
The "Bob-Tailed Horse!"

Now maybe you doubt
That he ever existed.
Or when being retold,
became--perhaps twisted.

No longer be doubters,
with tongue in your cheek.
As proof of the pudding,
leaves no need to speak.

For SISKIYOU ranged high!
way up on the mountain.
Kept mares closely checked,
continually a-countin'.

With wings on his hoof beats,
he's cavortin' about,
Over high ridges!
'n down into gullies no doubt.

His hoof prints remain.
The frog shows in track,
T'is planted like bronze,
that proves us a fact.

SISKIYOU roams the slopes!
on all of Mt. Shasta,
To this COUNTY so named,
to be retained ever aft-a.

He left his mammoth hoof prints
on SHASTA'S gorgeous flanks.
Ascendin' elevations!
paused, 'n jumped the RED BANKS.

Seeing horse tracks embedded,
showing so plainly in view.
Becomes meaningfully clearer,
as brought into focus, anew.

They're so plainly emblazoned,
'n clearly engraved,
On the side of MT. SHASTA,
to be forever enslaved.

By a horse of great size!
'n made to perfection.
You turn 'n look back,
for a glimpse, a reflection.

A bright Buckskin was SISKIYOU,
his hide shown as gold
On that snow misty morning,
when he was foaled.

When sun rises, spots still
glint through the trees,
Reflecting his presence,
upon the crystals of freeze.

Living out his long life,
way up high on the slope.
His shadow seen drifting,
among clouds as they float.

You'll know him for sure,
by his bobbed off tail.
'Tis like a rudder he uses,
to guide and sail.

It's kept worn short
from braking quick stops
Lowered like a flap,
as he descends and drops.

This he soon learned,
when by accident shorn
Back on that beautiful spring
'n sunny morn.

Shasta Valley below,
caused his statue of stance,
His moment's hesitation,
in flight from his prance.

He became completely entranced,
'n stopped to view,
Let his flying black tail
get tangled into...

OLD WHITNEY'S avalanche,
'n glacier's cold jaw,
As roaring sliced past
his rear, during a thaw.

Behold! Tail bobbed off,
in the wink of an eye,
Long before he could bolt
upright into the sky.

So never again will you see
his flowing tail long,
As he gracefully maneuvers,
with muscles so strong!

SISKIYOU will remain always
with a bob to his tail,
And legends keep flying
as he gallops the trail.

In blizzards and snowstorm,
all fine weathers blend
In SISKIYOU'S OWN COUNTRY,
in peace on the wind.

A horse with iron hooves
of the hardest of steel,
And endurance built in,
like a furnace and wheel.

He's larger than Bunyan's Ox,
a breathtaking sight of awe!
May see his golden hide drifting
out side of Darwin's law.

Yes, he's BUCKSKIN!
Color of first breed of horse.
Agreed from all sightings,
to be that color of course.

His size 'n great strength,
acquired from his slaves,
We the people of SISKIYOU,
beliefs come in strong waves.

We're proud of our SISKIYOU,
a giant with love,
As he continues to watch
over us all from above.

If lucky, will hear him whinny,
in the dead of the night
As he soars through the mist,
to again disappear, out of sight.

"DUN'S DOZING"
Our Buckskins, Duns, and Red Dun colored horses catching a few winks in the early morning sunshine.

Photo By V. June Collins

Photos By V. June Collins

*"**Splash**," (Splash Down) A Dun pony named and owned by eldest Grandson, Greg Collins. Of an era when rockets were first being sent into orbit. Upon their return to earth, it was by way of an ocean landing. They were called Splash Downs. About as speedy as a pony might get, no doubt, thus the name. Splash is shown on the porch, always casing the joint, for extra dog or cat food to appease his appetite. For some time this place of ours was known, (with a smile) by the sign on the side of house that said, "NO RANCHO YETTA!" Years passed, planned and otherwise. Much was done in Joe MaGee fashion, (temporary permanent) sometime later to be redone, correctly.*
***"The Sleigh,"*** *Mr. and Mrs. Santa Clause rides in each Christmas Parade, after spends the rest of year on our 1980 remodeled front porch.*
*Here Jerry and I have resided since 1964, where we raised Buckskin horses until 1989, when we began liking the sound of "retire."*

## BUCKSKIN ACRES

### By V. June Collins

Apple trees of BUCKSKIN
standing along the lane.
Yellow-hued leaves of autumn
fill each golden vein.

The Elms are also yellow
of the brightest hue.
Splashed like paint and dripping
tiny drops of dew.

Trees have taken coats of leaves,
laid 'em on the ground.
Like boys in field playing hard,
up and throwed 'em down.

Poplars, 'cots and cherries
shiver in ragged disarray.
As BUCKSKIN leaves at our feet
have fallen down along the way.

Those BUCKSKIN OAKS are thick,
Dotted all around the hill.
BUCKSKIN horses like them.
Would like to eat their fill.

All grasses of spring 'n summer
has BUCKSKIN color chose.
Clumps 'n blades far scattered
across field and into rows.

Rye grass, starch stiff, in field,
Heads bent down for winter.
Fodder great for horse to eat,
Seems Heaven up and sent 'er.

All our BUCKSKINS are grazing
on dead grass out in the field.
Camouflage to match their hides,
like armor and their shield.

Coats are many shades of yellow,
BUCKSKIN, GRULLA, DUN.
Their shining tones reflecting
and glistening in the sun.

WHISPER WILLOW is dark as shade,
a pleasing blended tone.
While her WILO WINE, a grullo colt,
has color that's all his own.

SHOR'S enough buckskin cream
of the very richest kind,
With a stripe to trim her up,
runs dark along her spine.

SANN's bright dapple, flashy hue,
glints both gold 'n copper.
She is the nicest little gal
and is still a looker-stopper.

TANGO's in the foreground
taking everything in stride.
She has a yellow creamy gold
wrapped up into her hide.

SPLASH DOWN, a dun pony
Nearly as broad as he is long.
His curious, loving little spirit,
Plays back most like in song.

Often, call him Boney Pony,
Just because he is so round.
He can cover lots of country
Sort of truckles over ground.

Now, this notch we have carved,
"Rancho Bucksin Acres."
Seems for some time, had waited
Was just looking for us takers.

Photo By V. June Collins

COWBOY IN CABBAGE PATCH
(Labor Day weekend 1972)
By V. June Collins
Cowboy Severn's in the Skunk Cabbage patch,
Grabbin' off rest, left over to catch.

Waiting for lunch to be served up in style
By two lassies behind him, all of the while.

Soon cheese and meat slapped in between bread
Will go down the hatch as everyone's fed.

A glug and gulp of water to wash it all down.
Up there on mountain side, quite far from town.

Re-cinched saddles, headed back onto trails,
Are off to make camp before setting sun pales.

Carter Meadows the destination, plan in time, to gain.
As back astraddle, happy thoughts filled our brain.

Scatted off single file, with bellies plum full.
Just riders 'n ranchers, all dyed, in the wool.

Was a fork in the trail, to each, came a choice.
Some went one way, others tattled, by voice.

We dangled along with our tails to the wind
Two different directions, to gain the same end.

Photo By V. June Collins

Agnes Lemos, bringing up drag.

*One morning I awoke from an especially realistic dream, so much so that after breakfast I was compelled to sit down and write the following. I was at the old home place corral and pasture, visiting from one horse to another with much love, joy, and comunication between us. Many of the horses had been gone for years, yet so unbelievably real. They appeared to be as glad to see me as I of them.*

## BE HAPPY, BUCK-APPY

### By V. June Collins

Was busy visiting in a corral full
Of my many old equine friends.
Each horse I call by name 'n chat,
Inwrought in joyous memory blends.

While many of these horses
That went drifting through my dream
Were different breeds and colors
And one was half a team.

Learned to ride on Nellie Big.
Was wide as she was tall.
I'd kick 'n kick to make her trot.
Unconcerned, she'd walk was all.

When finally was able to sit aboard
And on her, head a cow,
Graduated to another horse
With more speed and cow know-how.

Nellie finally quit babysitting kids
Yet thoughts of her are kind.
She was building-block of riding,
As I started bareback on behind.

Horses filed apast and milled about,
Glad to have me around again.
Me, I'm elated to be so chosen
And feel likened to as kin.

Yet, all the time I spent conversing,
Was casting eyes about.
For a special horse was looking.
Would appear without a doubt.

I'm Buckskin raised and Buckskin bred
Deep down within my soul.
But also find have a hollow spot
Left there dangling on my pole.

I fish around and yank it out.
What do you guess is found?
Appaloosa fits nick so clear.
They're seen dancing all around.

Have had a yen for many years
To own a Buckskin-Appy Horse.
With yellow coat upon back.
Black spots on rump, of course.

But kinda smile, feel warm inside,
My eyes caress this dream.
Hordes of horses fill 'em up. Cast
Reflections on hides' glossy sheen.

When I awoke, felt almost cheated.
Still could feel soft coats on hand.
But soon glad this chance was given
By those milling herds and band.

They're still corraled upon my memory
As by name they pass review.
Some old friends of yesteryears.
Of course, a few of them were new.

They were all there to greet me,
Strangely, with nary a push or shove.
Could it be the spirit of Christmas
With her circling, peaceful dove?

There was Nellie, Jim and Brownie,
Mike, Dock, Red and Fox.
Yellow Merrylegs, my sister's horse,
With black mane, tail and hocks.

Monte, Midnight, Blaze, Burns and Fly,
With Big, my fathers horse.
Dustem, Buck, Peanuts and Jungles.
She was my first very own, of course.

Tango was my special mare.
Was around for 22 years to love.
A Buckskin gal that did her chores
Without one push or shove.

Buckskin, Whisper, filled a void.
Was perfection through her years.
When heart gave out, joined others.
Was hard to see through tears.

Along came Breeze, Sra 'n Song.
All cream frosting on a cake.
Dispositions with manners mild
That followed in the wake.

Now others own Buckskins, Topaz,
Nugget, Govina, Splash and Rye.
Short was stay, sad, so fleeting,
Of foals Fandango, Shadow and Pye.

While Sann, our Buckskin broodmare,
Keeps stamping buckskins out,
Ben, Jerry's buckskin gelding,
Is still a joy on any route.

A fetching wench is filly Tro,
A classy weanling, Dun.
She runs, shows her speed,
While yearling Dally joins the fun.

Now Pink is my new, Red Dun mare.
Have had her nigh unto a year.
She's up and carved herself a notch,
Pretty nearly close to dear.

Shore, we raised up through her years
'Til finally turning three.
My saddle horse with hopes destined
And quite special to me be

Her spots are faint, rather sparce,
But surely fills the bill.
She's the only one in the barn
That tips her manger out to fill.

She's a light Dun-Appy filly.
Wears black frosting as a trim.
Striped hooves, mottled mouth,
On eyes and ears black edges rim.

I take the time to keep this pair
A trackin' and a trailin'.
Climb aboard with grunt 'n groan,
Sure keeps my spirits sailin'.

Guess I'm horse crazy. I've heard
It used quite loosely when
One speaks of little girls
And some old horse tradin' men.

But a world without a horse, it seems,
Would be not a world at all.
So they're still kept out in pasture
And cooped up in the stall.

*I wrote this poem in 1975, during a particularly lengthy spell of frozen snow and ice on our north hillside on the trail up to the barn. I call it...*

## TRAIL CLASS

### By V. June Collins

Yes, bundle up warm 'n brave the hill.
From warmth of house takes a will.
Then up the trail, a slippery strip,
With defiant feet that try to flip.
Trail leads up, you grab the fence,
Stagger of steps, and sorta mince.
Rocks protrude, gain another grip,
Finally reach barn on zigzag trip.
All now fed, as in comfort they chew.
'Tis a downward path for feet 'n you.
Again grab fence, as feet each stray.
Both it seems want to go another way.
Just need to put long nails in soles,
Yet, spring's water might seep in holes.
To nail those feet, not hide on wall,
To keep one upright so can not fall.
Stop coming down hill like a nervous skier.
With all those antics, be a he-er, or a she-er
With a few prayers 'n words, not in psalms,
To just arrive at bottom, unruffled and calm.
Really it's a feat! Such a professional skill!
To not land pissel-end up, on side of the hill.
Finally gain the house, will pause 'til eve,
When again, must put arms back in sleeve.
FOR THEN WILL DO THAT VERY SAME DANCE.
UP THE HILL 'N BACK.
NOW REALLY, DOES IT MAKE ANY SENSE?
OR IS IT JUST A LACK!

*Taken from an episode in my busy life, about 1974.*

## PINK'S DAY

By V. June Collins

Severns' sent word to us, *"Moon's right."
Would be marking calves 'n cattle.
So readied Saturday's trailer load
Of horses, blankets, gear 'n saddle.

Now, my mare has a goofy name.
"Poco Dinky Dean," Registry reads.
I soon dubbed her PINK, for short,
A Red Dun line-back, of sturdy seeds.

Gathered Pink 'n Ben in stall
And gave 'em a curry comb rush.
Their long winter hair, so shaggy,
Looked little better after brush.

Found mud balls where cinch went
So pulled 'n cut away.
Finally got most of them off...
Out of path of old cinch's play.

Decided that, those few now left,
Would fit behind girth just fine.
So fed 'em both their evening meal
Now would be ready most any time.

Drove out about 15 miles in valley
To good friends Severns' little spread.
Unloaded our two Dun, wooly beasts,
While others, saddled up and lead.

*Moon right: When altering livestock, according to the light or dark of the moon, they bleed less.*

Sun was up, 'n morning rather cool,
What a great day to work 'n ride.
Soon, all ambling along down lane
Like fresh water following tide.

Again both Ben 'n Pink, feeling oats,
As usual, first ride in spring.
Neither cared to be told what to do.
Their bit champing, did fairly ring.

Pink has her days, 'n I have mine,
When she hardly ever breaks a rule.
Then I brag unto myself to have found
This rare and precious Jewel.

Today our communication, plum nil
All morning, we were buttin' heads.
I wanted her to stop the jazz!
While she rejected offer, dead!

Pink continued getting higher still.
Refused to think of settling down.
I rode her up 'n down the slopes,
Yet, hump in her back stayed around.

Were a few stragglers, low in field,
In dobby mud, plum soft 'n deep.
I offered to ride out after them,
To try 'n slow mare's prancing feet.

Lather foamed on her long hair.
She still gave me, "No! You never mind!"
Finally ended drag back to corral.
Would soon dismount 'n rest my mind.

Cattle were slowly passing through
Yon open, last corral gate.
Now we riders, gathered 'n gabbin',
Would tie up 'n work 'n wait.

Well PINK you'll say, had my number.
Had sized up situation, well 'n fine.
She thought time had sure arrived
To sit that old gal, upon her dime!

She gave one quick, high jumping leap!
All four feet left that thar ground.
I grabbed for that safety strap!
Started sucking myself, tightly down.

On the third jump that old bitch
Sure had unhooked both my boots.
Out of stirrups they came flying back!
I thought, you crazy old Dun coot!

My feet kept gaining altitude! I hung on!
Soon were headed back over to the ground.
Fist now near buried into collar bone
That showed knuckle imprint, I later found.

My feet hit kerplunk! In front of mare.
She stopped! Then appeared quite amazed!
I had kept my head from hitting first.
She looked at me, just sorta gazed.

My death grip then, wrenched from grasp!
The rest of me sagged down in wad!
I slowly got up onto my feet
Like an old mad cow that's on the prod!

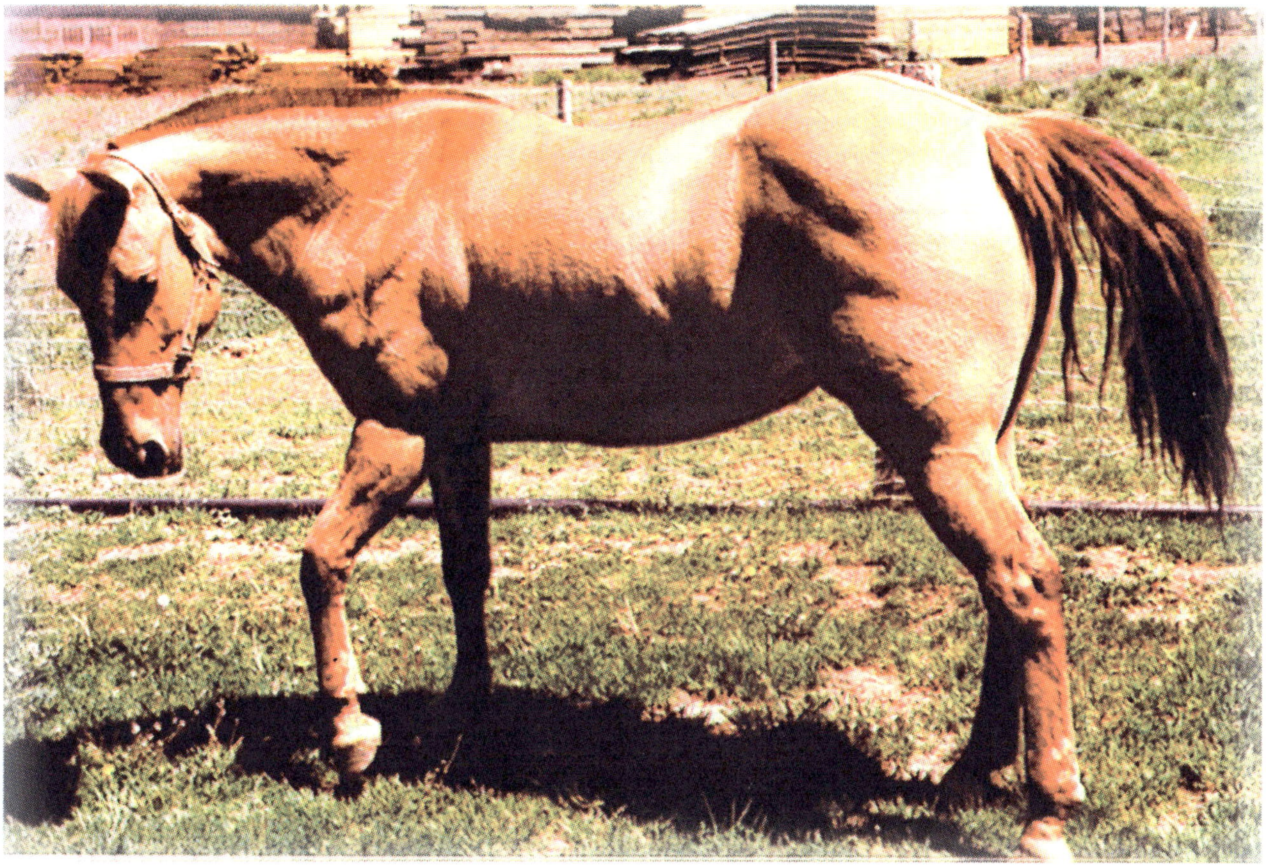

Poco Dinky Dean, "PINK"                                    Photos By V. June Collins

I gave her a few sound kicks in the slats!
Then started to clamber aboard, back on.
But quickly had another, pregnant thought.
Maybe those mud balls had done me wrong?

I now unloosened cinch, 'n sure enough!
Those balls had worked back underneath.
Was much like burrs under saddle blanket.
She had been hurting, beyond relief.

With pocket knife, I again whittled away,
Cut 'n pulled those rascals out!
Because, after marking 'n lunch time,
Would follow 'em back, out same route.

Maybe her belly yet still tender
When, in evening, mounted back up.
She still again had hump in back.
Could feel her muscles bunch 'n cup.

Each time she felt I'd relaxed,
She'd think, I'll try that again!
I'd sideways jerk her head to side
And gouge her sides into a spin!

She'd stumble round, near fall down!
Act dizzy, for just a minute.
Then she'd travel good a while.
Soon I'd see, her heart not in it.

Though straightened out for a time,
As to say, "That didn't work."
In a little while, old way returned.
I could feel her smile 'n smirk!

Back to barn in time, unsaddled.
Bid our friends a fond adieu.
All agree'd, had a busy day,
Plus enjoyable 'n true.

We loaded up 'n hauled 'em home,
Still disgusted with her stubborn way.
Bedded down for night, I was sorta puny
From jerks she'd put on display.

Next day we're to drive whole herd
About ten miles on to another pasture.
So awakened with a will, for sure!
But my way, sure felt no rapture.

My mind thought must come awake!
So early, but body would not get up.
I gave another poor excuse to rise!
Nothing worked! Must have frozen up!

I finally said to Jerry,--- Please!
As I stuggled 'n tried to sit up in bed.
You'll have to give me a gentle shove,
Cause I can now barely move my head!

I felt Ouch! Oh! So very tender.
All from hanging on, to not hit ground.
Not missed a spot! Even eye balls sore!
Couldn't bend! Solidified by pound!

Yes, I'm still vain, though not so proud
When it comes to tanglin' with the dirt!
At my age, have no qualms for sure.
Will pull leather to not get hurt.

In my younger days, to grab the horn
Sure took a lot of razz 'n guff!
I was a great deal more agile too.
A Ranch Jewel, carved out of rough!

Photo by Jerry Collins

V. June on "Pink ," Anderson, CA Horseshow

# HARRINGTON LAKE OR BUST

Photo By V. June Collins

A happening of Aug 20-1969. We hauled eight saddle horses, plus two pack horses approximately 100 miles into ELK VALLEY, south and west of HAPPY CAMP, CALIFORNIA, with plans of locating the old original pack trail between DEL NORTE and SISKIYOU Counties. We had made determined plans with the intentions of travel this long unused old trail, to the once-upon-a-time, extensively used, and overnight's stopping place of HARRINGTON LAKE. We would then spend our planned week's vacation in this paradise-like wilderness, many miles from civilization, fishing, bottle hunting and pure relaxed enjoyment. This trail was actively used by riders and pack strings, in early years, to bring supplies in from the coast and CRESENT CITY, inland communities, and YREKA during mining and gold rush years, lasting on into the 1930's.

The trail markings were dim and hard to follow at times. In other places, roots were worn nearly through from the many feet of horses and mules which had traversed its length in the past. We had a number of forced delays along the trail, while we again relocated old markings. We would all spread out and search for yet another visible mark, so as to again connect us to our destination. On one hillside we finally located a blaze on the underneath side of a large fallen tree which had appeared to be in the right direction. Re-marking and making our way along the trail was slowed in a number of areas, because of downed old-growth timber and from huge slides, which carried away entire hillsides and swept trail into oblivion, and also from markers hidden quietly among dense new growth.

Those involved were: KEITH AND JUNE SEVERNS and young grandson, CODY CURRIE, LAEL AND CAROLYN COLLINS and son GREG, AND JERRY AND JUNE COLLINS. Cody and Greg were 7 years of age. We had three young green, horses on this excursion, that had never been to the hills before. BRONZE, SANN, GOVINA. This is ever a caution. Flatlanders are apt to have a problem or two, but hopefully not get someone injured in the process.

Photo By V. June Collins

Ready to leave Elk Valley base camp-- On Left are Sann, her first time as pack horse for this trip, (a good experience for all green horses.) Carolyn Collins on Govina; Lael Collins on Tango; V. June Collins on Bronze. On the right, are Greg Collins on his pony, Splash; Rocky the pack horse in background; as is Jerry's horse Nugget; Cody on Popcorn; June Severns on Chuck.

Photo By V. June Collins

Our forced nights camp along the way.

Morning came, smoke drifted by, and coffee filled the air. Keith the early riser, had sour-dough cakes for bill a fare.

From the left- June Severns; Greg Collins; Jerry Collins; Keith Severns; Cody Currie; Carolyn Collins and Lael Collins. The horses shown grazing in background and also enjoying the solitude are Sann, Tango, Govina, Popcorn, and Chuck.

Photo By V. June Collins

This little bear is only one of a number we saw during the trip, which made us aware we needed to swing our groceries out of reach when not at camp.

*The next day we spent all afternoon away from camp of Harrington Lake, exploring the surrounding area, horseback. We saw larger black bear quite close, to all our enjoyment. When we got back to camp that evening, Cody remarked with enthusiasmn, "I saw a bear, and I wasn't even lying."*

# WISTFUL WILDERNESS

By V. June Collins

This little verse relates a trip
And a memory-refresher serves.
Old bottles filled our thoughts
As screwdrivers salved nerves.

We numbered eight, with horses ten.
To HARRINGTON LAKE or bust.
With spirits high, a week to spend,
This became another must.

We saddled up and packed our gear,
Left ELK VALLEY far behind.
As sounds of 'Powder River,
Let 'er Buck' echoed along line.

Pack horses, taut and fresh,
Seemed glad to be on trail.
Up, up we climbed a steady pace,
On a crooked narrow scale.

SPLASH DOWN became careless,
Crowded in too close behind.
GOVINA thought, watch your manners,
With a hind foot, did unwind.

Three short rounds she fired away,
A sound one to the chest.
As he wheeled away, she landed one,
To GREG's shin-bony crest.

Trail disappeared into space
In another chasm deep.
Only way now to get on by
Was to cut a pathway steep.

With axe 'n brawn they carved anew,
JERRY, KEITH and LAEL,
A detour for pack horses to trod
This narrow-gauged trail.

BRONZE became the new lead horse.
Looked for spooks at every turn.
A rock raised up in front of him.
He reached for sky like measuring-worm.

Trail was not made for passing.
For sure, no turnaround.
His hind feet took down the slope
Before his front feet found the ground.

This shook up those in line a bit.
It happened too fast to think.
I felt like lead in a sling shot
As around he spun on brink.

Decided it was too late in day.
Should return to meadow past.
Reversed direction, started back.
ROCKY, a pack horse, coming last.

Now ROCKY's a sturdy horse.
His black hide shone in sun.
He kept trying to let us know
He'd had enough, was done.

He was discontent and crowded in.
His pack, on side had slipped.
JUNE called, "It's gonna go!"
KEITH 'n I bailed off before it flipped.

"There he goes!" came in another breath.
Then over and over he went.
Down the hill in a willow patch,
Momentum crashing bent.

First his feet then the pack
Would flash around in view
To disappear and return again.
Seemed spun around and flew.

He thrashed around, plunged out of sight.
On down incline steep.
We seemed suspended, held our breath.
He lay there in a heap.

Only when quiet had descended
Could KEITH unhook the cinch.
ROCKY scrambled to his feet
Without the need of winch.

He struggled up onto the trail,
A mighty tuckered horse.
Made us all shake our heads.
So glad 'twas no remorse.

We tugged 'n grunted pack-gear back.
Every thing was fine.
Nothing broke but spirits.
Just took a little time.

KEITH hysted it out of gully-hold.
Was then relayed by JUNE.
I grabbed aholt 'n dragged away
Before the rising moon.

We re-packed ROCKY in the dark,
Then back to meadow went.
He seemed fine, in flying style,
Without a scar or dent.

Staked out horses, had some chow.
Boy, was old bed good!
'Twasn't very long until
We all were sawing wood.

When morning came smoke drifted by.
Coffee filled the air.
KEITH, the early riser,
Had sourdough cakes for bill of fare.

'Twas decided some green horses
Could use a little rest.
To scout out trail ahead today,
On foot, it seemed the best.

So CAROLYN, LAEL, KEITH 'n JERRY
Put fishing poles in hand.
Started out rebrushing trail
Through this wild 'n woolly land.

'Cause it held privacy real dear,
Grasp on with clenching fist.
Humans seldom trod this way.
For the bear, we'd not be missed.

Now CODY, GREG, JUNE S. 'n I
Held down this camp all day.
Cleaned 'n made a trickling spring.
Watered horses by relay.

Evening brought the wanderers back
With fish to fry for morn.
Screwdrivers sizzled down the hatch,
As did the horn-of-corn.

Morning dawned, we again re-packed,
Soon were headed out.
Traversed in single file the miles,
A new-blazed 'n steady route.

Lush green solitude greeted us.
Bear heaven, in a mirror.
The lake was glad to see us,
Motioned, to come a little nearer.

So off with packs, we made our camp.
Horses grazed nearby,
The only nature noise we had
Was the giant horse's fly.

Voices soon broke the calm
With yips of delighted glee.
Fishing tackle flipped about,
As you could plainly see.

Round rings on water surface
Was dimpled by feeding fish.
Sizzling tasty morsel. Thoughts
Started forming in a wish.

Our supper meal was bound to have
Rainbow in the pan.
This for sure was a feast
For each woman, boy and man.

Made beds, got snuggled down.
Soon as cozy as can be,
When brother bear came into camp
To see what he could see.

RUFF knew bear was out of bounds,
On his path a walking.
PEPPER woofed, REGO chimed.
Gave support to wild bear stalking.

Each horse fussed, stomped about,
Trembled in his hide.
Now brother bear sniffed so loud,
Our eyes came open wide.

RUFF finally had enough of this.
Must frighten him away.
So chased his heels over top of hill,
The rest of night to stay.

Breakfast ate 'n chins wiped off,
Horses up we gather.
To look some country over,
We all decided when 'n whether.

We saddled up 'n rode some trails.
CODY spied a bear.
CHUCK 'n BRONZE reared up their heads,
Started sniffing in the air.

Now JAKE'S back was tender.
The night in camp we hove.
He was turned out loose to follow,
To graze around 'n rove.

KEITH rode him 'n led the pack
Most of all the way.
He now felt real important.
Wasn't foolin' with acts of play.

On hind feet stood, bared his teeth,
Front feet flailed the air.
He meant, "Stay way on back,
This is my special share!"

We dug around a cabin old
For treasurers found like games.
Where porch once stood, was buried plank,
Carved with date and names.

Hand made coat 'n hat hooks,
Must have welcomed all travelers in.
When we exhausted all our efforts,
These momentoes were glad to win.

Saw another bear in the trail
As we were nearly back to camp.
Scampered out of sight in foliage,
So lush, sweet, cool 'n damp.

We'd swung vittles high in tree
In case one lurked around.
Were quite relieved, when into camp,
Nothing was strewn on ground.

We took a swim, some had baths,
Refreshed ourselves in sun.
Relished the glory of open air
Of this wilderness we'd won.

Arose at the break of day,
Was back on trail by eight.
Horses packed 'n straddled,
Strung out in homeward gait.

Rode five hours to lake on top.
Horses backs were hot.
Stripped packs 'n saddles off,
Glad for luncheon stop.

Munched 'n chewed sandwiches down,
Lolled around in shade.
Short while aroused, revived again,
As chance for nap did fade.

Saddle blankets seemed cool as ice,
As back on backs must go.
Lacked some cinch's tightness
As we pitched off down below.

Down south side of ELK HOLE,
All braced for our descent.
Hoof carefully picked each spot,
To balance as down we went.

GOVINA'S saddle started slipping.
CAROLYN, baled onto the ground.
Saddle bags flipped over top.
Around Govina's ears were found.

She objected to blindfolds so big,
Covered up her hearing.
She bucked 'n tried to free herself.
Fell down the hill, a rearing.

For a minute she lay in surprise,
Then over and over she flopped.
Saddle 'n cinch wore like collar
Down around her knees. She hopped.

JERRY finally overtook her dash,
Slashed out, cut latigo free.
Blood was flowing down her side.
Had rolled over a snaggly tree.

Scalped 'n skinned in many a spot
But must go on before she's sore.
For the pull back out other side
Still was one mighty chore.

Switched latigos, right to left,
The short one for a long.
Tightened up this old saddle down.
Pushed onward without a song.

Again crossed mire 'n started up.
Bluffs towered high above.
Slowly up, then stopped to rest.
Watched rocks, should horses shove.

With much relief, gained top,
Looked back with all thanksgiving.
Thanked each our lucky stars,
Yes, to be among those living!

JERRY said, "I've not lost a thing.
No need to retrace one step."
We all agreed his thoughts were ours
And sure sounded pretty hep.

Clipped off the miles back to base
With many scenes of splendor
CHIMNEY ROCK stood like a guard,
So straight, tall and slender.

ELK VALLEY was the haven
Nine hours had brought us to.
Horses neighed their pleasure,
As it slowly came in view.

We celebrated this arrival
To a justly pleasant spot.
Then spent another day absorbing
The beauty of the plot.

Again came time to trailer horses,
Over road and fill.
Down the crooked roadway,
Down the mountain 'n the hill.

The dust oozed in to every pore
Of each assorted, colored horse
And left them all a dunny gray,
A well-matched group, of course.

Soon put them in pasture.
They acted rather glad.
But now our vacation was over.
This left us kinda sad.

I've read this memory over.
It didn't give one hint
Of three other good horses
That didn't make the print.

Little NUGGET is a mixture
Of both chestnut 'n bay.
He really pulled his load along,
Willing all the way.

TANGO is a grandma,
A good Buckskin, you can bet.
She is a mountain horse supreme,
The best you'd ever get.

Sann is Buckskin also.
Her first time to haul a pack.
She put her shoulder to the wheel,
Took up all the slack.

I was really proud of her,
Worked honest all the while.
Carried all that was asked of her
In soft and easy style.

Now that they've been mentioned
My conscience had a lift.
With a bouquet of gratitude,
I wish to send to each this gift.

Sharing
Sun, Shade and Shadows of Summer!

Photo By V. June Collins

Along the trail, in 1972, on Chief Joseph 100 mile, Appaloosa Trail Ride, from Spencer Idaho, to West Yellowstone, Montana. Keith Severns on Timber, Jerry on Arrow and June Severns on Chief.

Jerry for the first ten years, of these rides, rode Arrow. He was a very , willing, and no nonsense kind of trail horse. His congenial abilities allowed these rides, and night camps, to become special remembered treasures.

Photo By V. June Collins

1973, Chief Joseph Trail Ride. June & Jerry's hats spent a night along the trail at Nez Perce Creek, perched on a ready made pine tree, hat rack outside their tent.

The Chief Joseph Trail Riders left Base camp on the Madison River in West Yellowstone, Montana, following the historic, Old Fountain trail to the Nez Perce Patrol's Cabin. We lunched at pine flat along the trail. We then took the Nez Perce Creek trail, and camped along Nez Perce Creek the first night. We rode on next day, to the Merry Mountain Trail, and nooned at Mary Lake, and in the afternoon rode on until late in evening, to the Otter Creek Campground and Camp for the second night. We followed the spectacular Yellowstone River across to Haden Valley, into Firehole Valley, and down Pelican Valley. Then down Pelican Creek, and we camped the third night at the northeast corner of Yellowstone Lake. We bathed at Pond Lake nearby. The trail from there took out the next morning, east across Mist Creek Pass, each horse was loaded with rider's gear, for two day's and a night. Pack horses brought in supper and breakfast and the last day's lunch. Finally, we made camp that evening in a nice meadow on Cold Creek, near where it emptied into Lamar Creek, our last nights camp out. That evening we watched a spectacular horse stampede, when a park official informed us, "No tying to trees." Wow!

   The next morning we followed the narrow, steep trail up and out of Mist Creek, dropping down into Miller Creek to the Lamar River and down the Lamar River into the valley, to Lamar Ranger Station. Here, all the rigs had been taken for the week, to wait out the return, of we riders and horses to claim them.

*Story in verse, of Jerry and June's second year ride. Taken from the ninth segment of first go round, on Chief Joseph, Appaloosa 100 Mile Trail Ride.*

## YELLOWSTONE APPY'S

By: V. June Collins:

**August, 1973**. Sat. 11th
Along Madison pitched our tents, on Chief Joseph Ride and start;
Separated gear, pondered, 'tis where vehicles and horses part.
Some chatted, renewed acquaintances, from many rides before,
Others fed and watered horses, before, tied them fast and sure.

Gathered up our envelopes from Janie Nash's bulging files;
We read the rules of what to do, along those many miles.
Missed Frank and Maxine Kramer, bad luck befell them both,
Nash's took up some slack, where ever was needed most.

Janie was filling Maxine's shoes, Kramer's wore them well,
Lyman, herded hay bales around, as Frank had for quite a spell.
Idell Moore hove into sight, with "Sizzler" close behind,
Unloaded, made her camp, saddled and rode before she dined.

Keith and June soon appeared and camp beside us made;
Told a few Royal Purple jokes, some to deep, too wade.
Lay our heads upon pillows, excitements soothed to sleep;
Some dozed off immediately, while others counted sheep.

Sun. 12th:
Sunday fresh of morning, breakfast we gobbled down;
Camp gear for week, was left piled upon the ground.
Heard round 'm up, head 'm out, vehicles form in line,
At Lamar destined to spend a while, quietly waiting out time.

Soon back to camp, on buses bold, an Appy cheery crew,
With appetites to match smiles, with greetings old and new.
Does Bob Harney wield wicked stick, barbecuing beef?
Does he wear his hat in glory, like another noble chief?

I asked to take his picture as his Porker rolled around,
He said, "I'd have to wait my turn, as if a celebrity I'd found."
Rode horses across river, between Madison's shallow shores,
To other side, through timber, on green carpeted, grassy floors.

Then back across her waters and down the other side,
Into camp and tied up horses, each within their hide.
The cooks again, have made a meal, quite fitting for a king;
Started quaying up in chow-lines, dinner bell toots, a ring.

With bellies full, much content, some chat and rest or sleep,
While others start to ready selves, for foot stompin' beats.
Limber up and liven up, those many horse ride 'n boots
Shouts, whoops and hollers 'til ten o'clock curfew toots.

Then off to bed, to sleep real fast, before another day awakes,
Feed mounts, pack up gear. What good smells coffee makes!
### Mon. 13th
Monday morn' dawned loud and clear, chow time filled air,
Settled down, with nose-bagged horses, lined up for bill afair.
Trail Boss "Tuck," on Buckskin Appy, is champing at the bit,
Will hurry up, get on horses, to see if your saddles fit.

One thing for sure as day wears on, you're bound to re-adjust;
While horse and rider becomes as one, like pie within its crust.
The tender spots toughen up, some brawn replaces fat,
Don't give a second thought, unto the two seats, upon you sat.

Saddles cinched, bridles on, first day's ride, comes true;
Stashed bed roll 'n duffel bags, to be gathered up by crew.
Spotted are the bottoms of this Appaloosa breed
And scattered on bodies like garden filled with seed.

Flowers along a garden wall all color, shade and hue;
The riders shirts and horses, an exciting thing to view.
At 9:30 left the Madison, then up, up, a steady climb,
Lodge Pole Pine 'n grassy glades, were with us all the time.

Much altitude we gained, a thousand feet and more;
Stopped for blows along way, up from valley floor.
Lunch stop at 12:30, in Pine Flat along the trail,
Unsaddled, hit the brush, like pony express' mail.

On Fountain Trail came down stairs, switching forth and back;
Stepped down into creek of Thistle, again take up some slack.
Then out into the open, as if some one had raised the blind;
Fountain Meadows, lay before us, left our trails of dust behind.

Down across Fire Hole River, our stirrups dipped its crest;
Horses wanted much more water, soon urged them on for rests.
The Patrol met us at River Crossing, escorted us off to camp
Skirting ridges and crossing roads, were like cattle down a ramp.

Day entwined, until eve surrounds, past lodge poles left and right.
Made our camp at Nez Perce Park, soon readied for the night.
Had our baths in Nez Perce Creek, was shallow, mild and wet;
Ate and danced beneath the moon, had a good time, you bet.

Tues. 14th:

Tuesday morn was on the trail at just about nine o'clock,
Single file, all strung out, with Appy tails above each hock.
Genie Mac rode spotted mule, in her regal, sort of style,
With calm collected manner, built in throughout the mile.

On trail of Mary Mountain, it lead us by her lake for lunch
Unsaddled sweaty horses, as cooled their backs a bunch.
Grandeur swelled before our eyes, unlocked our fondest door.
Sights of splendor absorbed in souls, oozed into every pore.

A trail rider's dreams about, and hope realized, in the flesh;
Distant landscapes far reaching, all so lush, green and fresh
Visions soared, filled our sights, beyond ones greatest dream,
Engulfed our inner being, was entwined 'round all we'd seen.

Buffalo herds upon the slopes. Aged bull resting in the timber.
A grouse, sat stiff, stark, and still, most anything but limber.
Another herd of Buffalo was seen escaping through woods;
Gathered up cows and calves, ceased chewing of their cud's.

Many bog holes crossed our trails, a few horses disapproved,
Some passed like as every day, while others double grooved.
Down my path there lay a log, most certainly, not high;
My ol' Blue hoss, put down his head, gave it all his eye.

Gave him slack to step across, was as polite as I could be.
He reared his front feet into air, nearly planting me in a tree.
Finally bedded down on Otter Creek, for second night of rest;
Chowed our horses, made camp, sound of dinner call was best.

On other side of camp forced to pack gear, a very long ways,
Made us late getting onto line, though had not stopped to graze.
Crawled into bed, much to my surprise, whole knee black & blue,
Seems when becoming near unsaddled, canteen had banged me too.
Wed. 15th:
Awakened early, to white, frosty morning, painted all silver white
Very few sat at table benches, was a breakfast stand up, plight.
Those that did, left prints of warmth, rears looked mighty cold.
It took a strong and daring heart, with courage rather bold.

Patrol led way across highway and on over Chittendon Bridge
Yellowstone River raging below, then we lined out for the ridge.
Calls of close ranks, tighten gaps, came up and down the valley.
By Stanger, and all other scouts, our soldiers on their sally.

Saw fishermen in their wader's, casting out their flies for fish.
Calls like "Indians" echoed back, in good luck, answered wish.
Spiraled up onto a bluff, far above the rapids of Yellowstone,
Sight below, took breath away, watching writhing waters groan.

At Lake Yellowstone made camp, upon her grassy, N. E. rim
Bathed in pond beside her, and emerged clean, fresh and trim.
Old moose cow and calf came down, for a sip of waters crystal dew,
Disappeared back up bank, before much grass, she chanced to chew.
After supper, pins were given, to those dedicated riders few
Who'd made 5 and 9 year rides, we clapped praises, into view.

Thur. 16th:
Woke up early come morning, to the dull, dull, crack of dawn;
Veil of mist hanging heavy, like dew blanket, upon a lawn.
Today must make division, all personal gear we would pack
Separate, only needed thing's, to put upon our horses back.

Our rain gear became number one, visions nudged us on
To be left wet and soggy, erased any thoughts of song.
We're asked to stay in single file, on new blazed route n' trail,
Horses hooves accomplish this, through wooded hill 'n dale.

Soon were lined out on trail, a bright clad smiling bunch.
Sun came out, shined a bit, long before, stopped for lunch.
A pleasant day was had by all, as up Mist Creek we twined.
Up and down the line was cheer, felt every thing was fine.

George's stance in saddle, always, visioned in our mind,
As he leads his pack horse, right along, close behind.
He never seems to hurry, as we pass him, along the trail,
Traveling on, is most every where, taking care of detail.

If shut your eyes and think a bit; He'll plainly come in view,
For he's been around Appy bunch, lots longer than me 'n you.
Camera crew covers lots of ground, out-distances horse 'n man.
Both walk and ride, with heavy gear-many times they ran.

At Cold Creek, Lamar River crossing, camp lay on other side.
Halt was called that echoed, so watered and rested horses' hides.
Then came strange orders, words, to each listening ear
No tying horses tonight! Just might mar trees or grass, a fear.

Confusion ran in waves about, from man to horse to crew.
Apprehension kept rising. Dread mounted! up and grew.
Trail horses quietly ate their grass, appreciating a time to rest;
Others never had tasted freedom, thought a romp far the best.

Liberty built excitement, rounded up all others that they could,
Back through camp thundered, over sleeping bags, as we stood
It soon became apparent, to the new one, placed in camps charge
Be mayhem before break of day, if all horse left out, at large.

Finally were told, could tie for night, a regular nights sleep could get.
With dish and spoon, lined up fast, for hot stew warmly het.
Fri. 17th:
Breakfast mush was ladled out, to fill our cold empty spaces,
Gathered and watered horses, each one found their places.
Trail climbed 'n narrowed, on mountain-side, waters below churn,
Horse tracks notched the outside edge, beyond a point of no return.

Relieved, as horses gain the other side, without a backward glance.
Halt was called, as those behind prayed, horses wouldn't prance.
An old cow moose out flanked our group, for miles she ran in line.
Eventually gained other side, she had ran a long and weary time.

In distance LaMar Ranger Station appeared, end of ride for year;
With grace of God, will again return, with Jerry, myself and gear.
At rigs we enjoyed a scrub, a change of cloths, final eve of parting
Ate, danced, laughed a lot, before in morn, all directions starting.

Perhaps gather in "74" at Lamar, another hundred miles devour!
Again, leave the trail out behind, with our "Appy Horses, Power."

*Most of us that write poetry have a few dog stories in our collections. This is one dog that made sure we would remember him.*

## SEVERNS' DOG, RUFF

By V. June Collins

"Ruff" is quite a shepherd's dog!
Has one keen mind, all his own.
Heels all critters on the ranch!
Bunched together and all alone.

We'd saddle up to leave the rigs
Yet old dog would never fail.
To nab a horse's heel or two
Before starting on up the trail.

Then you'd hear Keith loudly shout,
"You S of a B and Bastard dog!"
While laggard tried to regain his seat
Among rising dust, boiled up, in fog.

Ruff, with a rush, soon out in lead,
Pleased he'd gotten riders into gear,
Bides his time until rest or blow.
Nabs another unsuspecting heel, from rear.

He heeled those critters in the chute.
Hooves fluttered past a broken board.
As a prodder, great, he nimbly worked.
His deviltry he seemed to hoard.

One day while pushing calves along
In stops 'n spurts of gusty speed,
Calf decided to turn himself around.
Reversed direction... to succeed.

Keith clambered over side of top
To man-handle calf back in line
While Ruff was still eyeballing slot
For another heel to nip just fine.

Air had turned a wild, wild blue!
Keiths voice, came loud 'n clear.
Ruff not choosy what passed by.
Nailed Keith, as boots disappear.

Ruff quickly knew he's in trouble!
From that corral he left in haste!
Would again lay low, 'n bide his time,
For busy Boss had no time to waste.

Again in fall, camped at Carter Meadow.
The night turned shivery with frost.
Ruff jumped in back of Severns' camper.
Looked sad, like some old doggie lost.

Then Keith pulled down pad 'n sacks,
So old Ruff could curl up under rig.
He called and called one-minded Ruff
To come back outside, not into brig.

But old Ruff jumped up high in bed.
Defied him, with both snarl and snap.
This sure was the wrong thing to do
For Keith unwound, like doing rap.

Ruff was plum busy, switchin' ends,
Just savin' his unprotected rear.
Gathered up speed to maneuver.
His old confidence did disappear.

Their noise soon arose as thunder!
Keen yips, like lightning flashed!
Old Ruff was looking for cover.
Quickly, back outside he dashed!

Ruff sure knew his bluff's called.
Started headin' for most any shelter.
Now, door of Collins' rig hung open.
Bounded in scared, helter-skelter.

We had good laugh, there in lamp light.
Keith in hasty chase came into view.
Old Ruff had sure met his match.
His apologies just might be overdue.

Suddenly things had gotten out of hand
While this big fracas kept heatin' up.
Ruff just decided, Good Dog he would be
Instead of...   One Ornery Pup!

Photo By V. June Collins

June and Keith Severns at Olympic Stadium Mexico City, during the 1968 Summer Olympics.

What a good time we had!

To Keith Severns  4/5/75

# FRIEND OF FRIENDS
By V. June Collins

We proudly wave our salute to you, Keith.
Your absence sorrows, into sobs of grief.
Seeking, querys, we ask and wonder, Why?
Taken from us quickly, a very special guy.
Lives richer, having known your warmth and charm.
You're direly missed from this land, home 'n farm.
A bower of strength. Keith, a comfort sender;
Were rough, tough, loud, yet so very tender.
You were the West, the wind, the soft of snows.
Part of the summer's gentle breeze that blows.
Roar of truck motors, horns loud blasting toots.
The clatter of hooves in busy Rodeo Chutes.
Up rocky hill-sides, across deep, boggy mire.
Our horses on the trail, onto camp by the fire.
Lambs that came early, in cold of the spring.
The calves, the foals and birds in trees sing.
The dogs, the cats and the wind in the barn.
Clank of machinery, waiting roosters crow alarm.
A multitude of things entwined, all among us yet.
Quiet and lingering, to not soon forget.
Clasped, held dear, to our memory clings...
We'll miss intoned feel, on friendship wings.
In flight, soar aloft, from all those you touch
With magnetic attraction, embedded deep, so much.
Off on many rides, to be continued up in the sky.
We shall not forget you, nor shall we ever try.

We stray behind in thought.

*Yes, we traded a pair of peacocks to a fellow for a burro.*

## BEBE

By V. June Collins

Yes, we have quite a new addition.
Her voice is rather hoarse.
Fact, you might call it squeaky,
A sound of burro vocal chorus.

She's shy, yet doesn't miss a thing.
Would be to say, you're correct.
She hees and haws her anguish.
Same sound as with joy's dialect.

It has a sound that's in need of oil,
Yet, could be a favorite rusty gate.
She tunes in by ear, and on sight
When we appear or stand and wait.

We made big trade, one for another,
A pair of peacocks sealed the deal.
One was about as noisy as the other
Voice of burro is the best we feel.

Her love is tender, oh so catching,
As she nuzzles for more attention.
Yes, have a Burro in need of manger.
One to be built, I might mention.

We hang her hay up in a net.
In disdain, she pulls it out.
Paws it down into her bed
And soon scatters it all about.

She's a miniature, still looks a baby.
Is dubbed BEBE, like shot, for short.
Soft nose protrudes for caresses
While yon barn is now her fort.

Makes us smile with all her smarts.
Just puts our horses now to shame
For sure, she don't miss a bit.
Has snappy eyes and wild bushy mane.

There, too, is our Dalmatian, Tappy,

Still her happy friendly self,
As she smiles, as she says hello,
Like a warm and cheery elf.

A smile like a tooth paste add
As her ivories gleam and show.
Wiggles rump, taps her feet,
Then again is truly on the go.

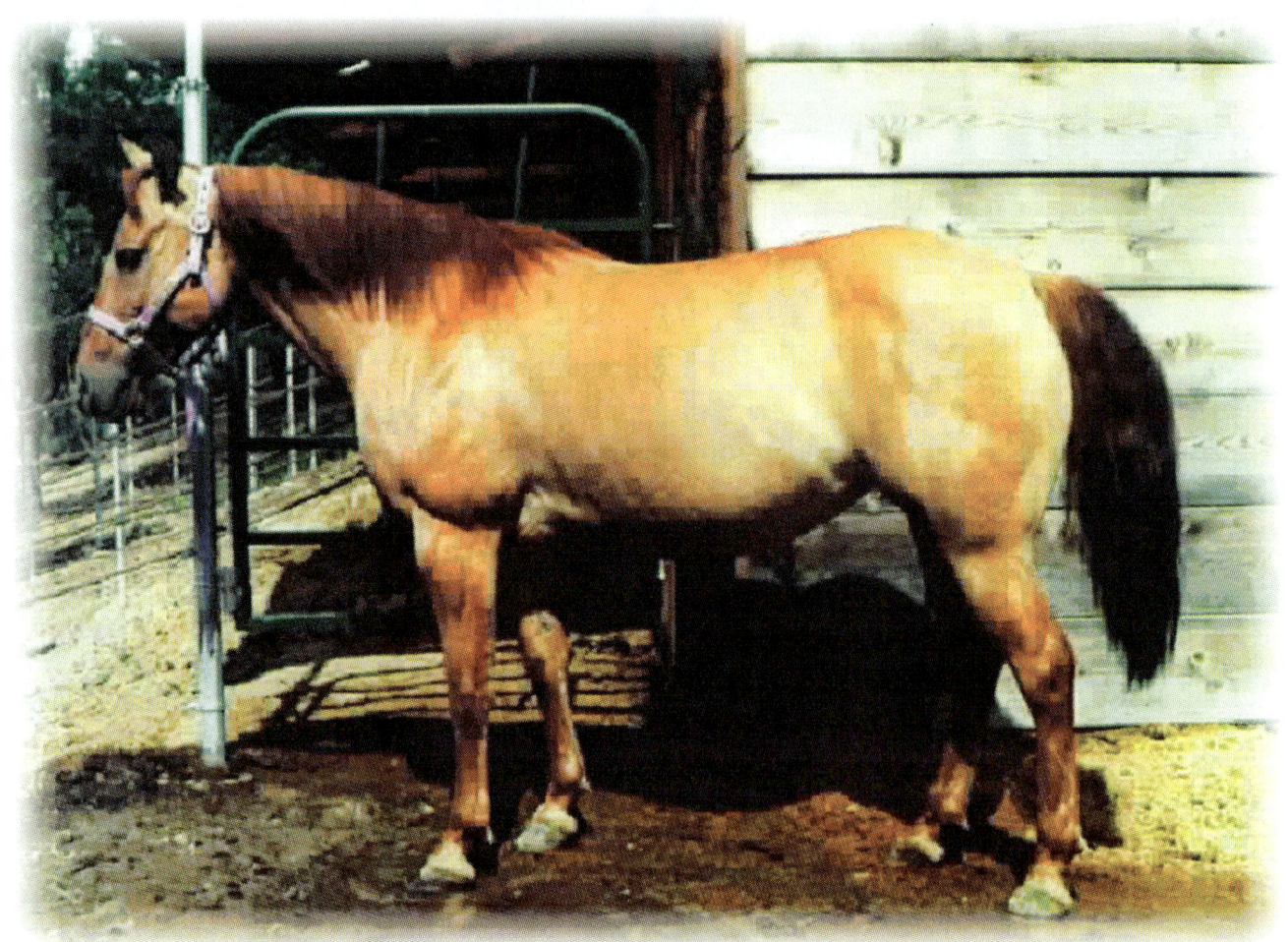

Photo By V. June Collins

"Pink," standing near the runways at the barn, which she was in during this happening.

*A rememberance of a happening, some years back, to my Red Dun, Quarter Horse, mare. She has the silly registered name of POCO DINKY DEAN. I call her "PINK." The Poem is so dubbed.*

PINK'S CALL

V. June Collins

Have had a Case loader many years.
It stands fair to middlin' tall.
Have gotten lots of use from it.
Helped me clean up in each stall.

It's rather chuffy, about 4 feet.
With its bucket, scoops a bite.
We, through doorways, then nudged.
Somtimes worked far into night.

We trundled on off to dump bank,
Using separate space each year.
Just so don't transplant worms
Onto pastures, where they'd adhere.

Then it sets, for another season,
Before, as fertilizer, goes on the grass.
That way not planting worms into
Our horses bellies, so extra fast.

One day was cleaning up by hand
Around the edges of the stall.
Pink, every little while, whinnied
And to me, would call.

She's a rather independent mare.
Will turn her head, most in disgust,
Many times when I wish to pet her,
Feel her saying, "Okay! If I must."

I talked to her through the wall,
Called her lunch-mouth. It's not time.
Still, she softly nickered to me,
Didn't make much sense or rhyme.

I then lay down fork into the corner,
Must just talk to her face to face.
Was so surprised, as I greeted her.
I felt guilty, lowly, in disgrace.

On something sharp she'd rubbed head.
Top eye lid hung down, limp as string.
Across an open, staring eyeball
Eyelashes hung, like feathered wing.

That sad open eye was begging me.
Its white shone a circle all round.
Blood ran down across her lovely face.
Dripped off her nose and onto ground.

Now for about a half hour or so,
Had delayed attention, this I knew.
I swallowed hard, in sad remorse,
Felt her asking, "Help me too."

Often times then, was home alone.
And sun nearing time of going down.
I knew something quick, must be done.
Had to call Vet quite far from town.

Started backing up rig to trailer.
For he too, had not yet got home.
Loaded Pink for journey to Doctor.
Left our message upon Vet's phone.

Was nearly dark by time I arrived.
Doc brought cord and light to use.
Would have to lay her down on lawn.
And make her take a little snooze.

Attached some ropes in preparation.
For sweet dreams, gave her a shot.
Quite soon her knees began to buckle.
We eased her down on grassy plot.

As she lay there in prostration.
His attention now most deep.
I held the light, he stitched away.
Sews speedily while she's asleep.

Dr. Paul may not be a seamstress,
But man, he sure did one swell job.
Those stitches put her lashes back
Above eye, like kernels on a cob.

She soon stirred and lifted self
Upon each wobbly, unsteady limb.
Reloaded her with a thankful heart.
Things now did not feel so grim.

I hauled her back home to orchard.
Fresh water, filled her water tub.
Stuffed a haynet full of leafy hay.
Crossed-tied her, so couldn't rub.

Here in shade she'd spend some time,
Anchored between trailer and a tree.
So could not scratch her stitches
On water tub or bended knee.

Don't know if she ever figured out
Why not allowed to eat from ground.
She could neither reach the tree
Or corner of trailer to rub around.

All things it seems were off limits.
For brisk rub or soothing swipe
Not one easy thing to accomplish.
Was almost hog-tied, in her plight.

Yes, her eyelid grew back smoothly.
Only a few white hairs tell the tale.
There to remind me of a happening
From my saddle mare's history trail.
(*One verse added at* 1996 *Cowboy poetry show*)
**This spring, she turned 30 years.**
**'Tis like 90, on humans' charts.**
**Enjoy her in barn and out in pasture.**
**Still, God allowing us not to part.**

Now more years have slipped away
As appeared, quite early, 2002 year.
On 7th day of June, to be exact...
Pink found no longer, could adhere.

Age equal to 102 in our years of time.
While she got skinny and very slow,
Our memories tally up, reaching many,
Always, still hard to let go, you know.

*I received my Crook County Historical Society, June 1990 publication which included a poem "Memories" written by Hazel (Smith) Denton, (a girlhood friend of early treasured years.) It was written of neighboring families and places which included the Blevins', my family, during late 1920's and 1930's. I was about 11 years of age. My mind played back in time. Soon I was compelled to write the following, which she too, was a part of.*

*Photo by Isaac M. Blevins*

*In winter of 1926. V. June at 11 years of age, on Jungles. Mare given to her by grandparents, (Coe and Pa) Cora & Ike Blevins, when ten years old.*

## OCHOCO'S MEMORY RENDEZVOUS

V. June Collins

I read Hazel's verse "MEMORIES"
With much feeling and happy thought.
The past rose up and welcomed me.
Savored well, those days we'd caught.

OCHOCO MEMORIES stirred and flooded
Filled crevasses to the very top.
That day I rode my little mare, Jungles,
Jigging down roadway klippy-klop.
From my home at OCHOCO STATION,
My happy thoughts now in tow.
On to Smith Mill, a busy place,
Where I so often chose to go.

Trotted in pleasure, three miles or so
Where Hazel 'n Thelma's family lived.
I wanted Hazel to come spend the night,
Begged her mom, yet little did she give.
She replied, "No. No. Not tonight!
So much time, you two spend together."
We followed her around about her chores,
And plied her with  Why? 'n Whether?

Her mom finally had a fast duty call,
To yon out-house, below facing bank.
We perched ourselves upon the slope.
A sudden light glowed, in form of prank.
We dashed down quickly, turned the button
On outside of that old door's frame.
Her mom was our prisoner now, so caged,
And we, in the driver's seat of fame.

We called out, "You'll have to promise
That, if 'n when we let you out,
That Hazel can come for night's stay.
And will be neither whips or shout."
She finally said, "OK, You can go!"
So we then let her out gently, free.
She smiled, we knew her word was gold.
We were both smiling in happy glee.

Blevins' later moved away, time gone by.
    Probably forty years past, or more.
We're back for pioneer picnic pleasures
    And all visiting like door to door.
I spotted Sylvia, Hazel's mom in crowd.
    And worked my way up close and near.
Put arm around her shoulders 'n whispered,
    "Been locked in out-house lately, Dear?"

She looked up, with a gasp of glee!
    "Oh, June," words came quick and fast!
Her memory knew only one such person
    That fit description, back in our past.
Many memories, I too, hold 'n treasure.
    OCHOCO has a very dear 'n special ring.
Lookout Mountain echoes, long refrains
    Which fill the mind, replay 'n sing.

Our neighborhood built on solid ground.
    One's word was held strong and fast.
Were you to meet another on a divide
    Was sacredly kept 'n meant to last.
All knew when another's word was given
    That, like gold, was sure and right.
To lie, would be the same as steal,
    Your character flawed in all's sight.

Those days of much truth and trust
    When too, our doors unlocked 'n free.
Only to have lived in such world, special,
    Was but part of my early life, you see.
This in itself, a granted treasure,
    Though today for many has fallen short.
Are forced to bar doors with distrust,
    From fear of fellow mankind's sort.

Photo below: By V. June (Blevins)Collins with Gordon Garners camera, (ca 1931) This Photo came back to me, (July 1, 2000,) at our 60th Wedding Celebration in Yreka, as a "Smiling" reminder.

### On top of (4 door) Model A Ford:
 1. Gordon Garner
 2. Evelyn (Blevins)
 3. Velma (Keeton)
 4. Phronia "Sally" (Hinderman) Nentl
 5. Valoura (Work) Johnson Grubb
 6. Benjamin Henderman

### Clinging or standing on car back:
 7. Oma (Keeton)
 8. Thelma (Smith) Roberts
 9. Elva Mae (Keeton)
 10 Hazel (Smith) Denton
 11. Hester (Lanius)
 12. Verdon Garner, on ground involved in horse play!

Photo By Jerry Collins

**1980 Back row :** Phronia "Sally" Hinderman Nentl; Hazel Smith Denton; V. June Blevins Collins; and Thelma Smith Robertson.

Front row: Valoura Work Johnson Grubb; and **Silvia, Mrs Lon Smith**, Mother of Hazel and Thelma Smith.

and together again, July 17, 2000 lunch.

Photo By Jerry Collins

2000-Hazel (Smith) Denton
Sally (Hinderman) Nentl
Valoura (Johnson) Grubb- *(deceased) 2002)*
V. June (Blevins) Collins

Ochoco Rendezvous - Page 176  **Enjoy!**

Photo by David Lee Rose

SONNY CURRIE riding Cooley, with his dog Hought.

Sunny is a long time resident of Montague, California, the son-in-law of June and the late Keith Severn, long time ranchers in Shasta Valley. Their daughter Karen, Sonny's wife, has worked for Littrell Parts for many years. They are more like family.

Photos By V. June Collins

Boat dock near Camp Creek, where Sonny Currie wet his daly rope to catch a wiley cow in 1991. Pilot Rock on the Siskiyou Mountains can be seen in the background.

*Written from a situation on cattle summer range land, up the Klamath River along the Iron Gate reservoir. Like many other areas of today, it has many recreationalists on its shores, in mixed combinations. This true happening was born out of Sunny Currie's amusing experience.*

## CURRIE
### By V. June Collins

This story is built of spice,
"CURRIE" TO BE EXACT!
While many Curries make the list.
Will ramble on, in fact.
  Have curry brushes, curry combs
  Curry powder, too, comes to mind.
  Some are mild, some quite hot...
  Others leave ties, that bind.
We've heard it told in descriptions
Some characters, almost like a disease.
Even wild 'n wooly and full of fleas,
And never curried, below the knees.
  But this here feller, I have in mind,
  Sure will, drop a catchin' loop.
  At times every thing goes dandy.
  Other times, might end up, in soup.
SONNY CURRIE a friend of mine,
Can dab his lasso rope, real fine.
His story may sound exaggerated
While he spins both rope and line.
  CURRIE drives truck, five days a week,
  This puts beans upon their table.
  While rest of week, come Friday eve,
  Find it's neither a big yarn, or fable.
He rides and ropes, then, real hard
To fill his hours with pleasure.
They gather stock 'n practice skills
For neighbors, friends, 'n leisure.
  He's covered lots of miles in hills.
  Upon Klamath Reaches, is old hand.
  At riding, rolling brushy hillsides
  In scrub oak 'n over soapbrush land.

His gathering stragglers, in the fall,
Gives CURRIE 'n horse much joy.
Cows full of grass are most content,
Won't leave, for man, horse, or boy.
> Doggies settled deep down, in thicket,
> Quiet, trying hard, not to be seen.
> 'Til a day, CURRIE riding COOLEY,
> Found that heifer, like radar beam.

They'd sure caught her by surprise.
Quick, CURRIE dallied up his rope.
 Ol' gal, only had her escape in mind.
 Like arrow, Sunny dabbed his rope.
> She hit the end. COOLEY-GRUNTED!
> Sunny's saddle, whined and creaked!
> When, this ol' gal, gave it all she had
> Sunny's dally, smoked 'n squeaked.

Then it flew right on off, the horn,
It was just a flappin' in the breeze.
COOLEY leaped out, in hot persuit,
From CURRIE's, jabs 'n squeeze.
> They stayed real close behind her
> As rounded hill, down to the lake.
> Where campers and those boaters,
> In some relaxing pleasures, take.

Bovines usually, give these such camps
A wide birth, in attempt to disappear.
But this ol' gal had other ideas,
She was most wild-eyed, with fear!
> She dashed right through their camp,
> Gave little time for human flight.
> There, a bikini-clad, young lady
> Had appeared, in her line of sight.

Bikini, was standing on the boat dock
Next to where a boat, was also, tied.
Quickly, Bikini had to jump 'n scramble
From out of this line of traffic, spied.
> Ol' heifer, headin' for the boat-dock
> As she straightened out from bend.
> Her eyes fastened like a gunner sight,
> To that far side, open-gated, end.

Looked like someone had left gate open.
To her, would sure now, be escape.
She hysted tail, with burst of speed,
Right on off, into the depth of lake.
    To have that brute get plum away,
    From CURRIE, was hard to take.
    But to see his lasso, wave goodbye,
    Made his hackles rise and shake.
He fast, bounded off, on the run,
Fairly spinning of his wheels.
His spurs were wildly jangling,
Hanging on for life, to his heels.
    Ol' heifer, having plunged in deep,
    Was swimmin' for freedom's other shore.
    CURRIE threw reins to the Bikini gal.
    Into boat they took off, with roar.
Bikini's husband, over-took Ol' heifer.
Currie's lasso, was trailing out behind.
With thought in mind took her in tow,
As quickly, gathered up his line.
    They circled 'n headed back to dock
    With ol' bovine, paddlin' along behind.
    She's was beached in breathless fashion,
    Lay on shore a puffin', on end of line.
CURRIE then, got back on COOLEY.
And snuggly dallied up, his wet rope,
While OL' COOLEY was diggin up dirt.
He and Currie, fetched her, along the slope.
    This for sure, is hand made, true story...
    ABOUT A HALF-BRAHMA, SWIMMIN' COW.
    And how CURRIE wets his dally rope,
    WHEN HE CATCHES A WILEY COW!

# DON CAUBLE'S RUNAWAY GOLF CART

By V. June Collins

One time when meeting called in Sunriver,
Wives also joined fellows in that stay.
Boys busy attending meeting, before golf.
We girls were soon off to shop and play.

Black Butte tolled boys in for planned game
Don, Jerry, Lael 'n Ken.
They hit balls, some quite straight,
While others had a bunch of ben'.

Day wore on... then at number twelve
Don was driving a cart like pro.
He came a'zoomin' up to the green.
Was then, just anything but slow.

Ken was standing looking other way.
Probably thinking about coming putt.
He was indeed in line, in Don's path,
And cart hit Ken just below the butt.

Knocked him forward, face in dirt!
As he jabbed on gas for brake.
Was much like a steam roller,
Quickly was signing up his fate.

All too soon he was ironed out.
Run up his legs 'n onto back.
Decided to man handle cart off of him
As he, in shock, was lying like a sack.

Excitement was like an echo rising.
You could say it was sorta keen!
Ken slowly got up 'n wiggled self.
Man! Now he was turnin' mean!

What you tryin' to do? You jerk!
You might have killed me dead!
Don had become most speechless.
Seems could barely shake his head.

As Ken waved his arms 'n proceeded
To tell Don what was on his mind.
Don had once been in driver's seat.
It seems he quickly got on behind.

Well, after a bit, peace reigned again,
Their game continued on to end.
Finally, got to be the most amusing
As each added his version's blend.

Back and forth came jibs 'n jibes
Of each other's shipping skills,
Up 'n over those grassy knolls
And back down the knobs 'n hills.

Laughed 'n joked on into the ridiculous
While near-tragedy had been averted.
Wives joined them for dinner hour,
Story unfolded, their details, inserted.

It seems each time things all level off,
Someone opens up another can of worms.
Yes, will say, Friendship's are Golden...
And we're still on good, speaking terms.

# COWBOY
## 6-6-97

By V. June Collins

Each cowboy's worth, we here honor
In their rough, and rugged, just cause.
They rode ahead, paved a way into valley
To them, we clap our loud applause.

Riding herd, while their cattle scattered
Brought for valley's future, on the hoof.
Homes, and barns were later built
A shelter beneath, each covered roof.

To this way of life, called independent
Where hungry cattle calls, to be fed.
All forced to endure winters, bitter cold
While storms linger long-- overhead.

Cowboys with their many faithful horses
We feel in depth of heart, belong to stay.
We honor Shasta Valley, and her cowboys
In arms of our valley, gathered here today.

Siskiyou County Cowboy Poetry reciters and performers efforts, finally paid off by allowing them to honor the Cowboys of Siskiyou County, past and present, with a larger than life statue. (A Cowboy astride his horse with calf slung across saddle in front of him.) It was made and designed by Yreka's unique artist, Ralph Starritt, and Dedicated April 6, 1996 at Montague, CA Railroad Park.

The Blue Goose, Excursion, Train, Yreka to Montague and back, make's its noon turn around here during its summer runs.

Photos by V. June Collins

Photos By V. June Collins
Ralph Starritt, Artist standing in front of his creation, with mother "Min" Starritt, shortly after the dedication ceremony, April 6, 1996.

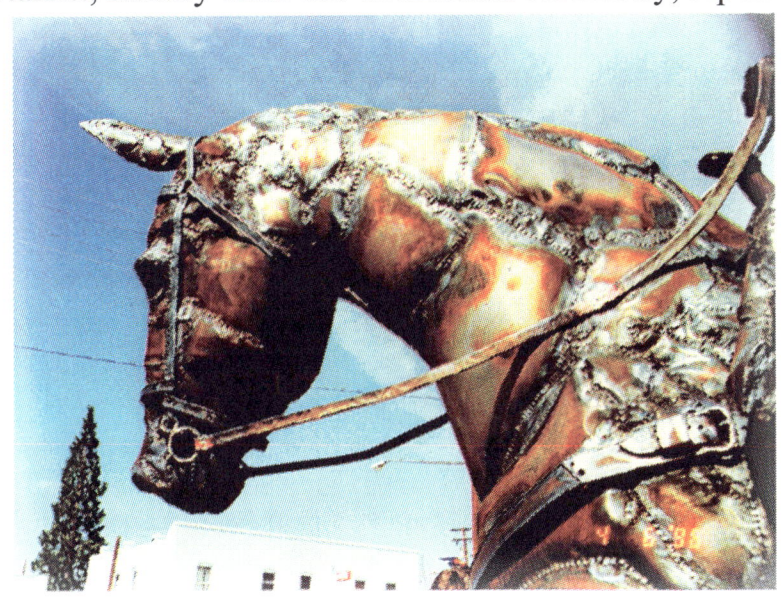

Ralph has done many interesting pieces in Yreka. "The Miner and Mule" at the center off ramp that welcomes you into town. "The Fireman and Dalmation dog" on Miner Street in front of the fire hall. In the entry-way at Miner's Inn Convention Center, is a special wall piece to be admired. Also going north, on I-5, between Grenada and Yreka an over-sized cow graces the country side. On entering Etna a pack horse group is your pleasure. Other creations to grace our communities is a very large, buffalo and attention getting dragon to catch your eye. Ralph busily, welds and fashions his realistic, sheet-metal creations into existence. Often to become our pleasures and treasures to revisit.

*At The Community Theater in Yreka, California, in 1991, during the Cowboy Poetry program, a fellow reciter, ROY SMITH, said to me, "Do you know, you rock when you walk?" I laughed! and replied, "It has something to do with age." This poem is a product of those after thoughts.*

## ROCK 'N WALK

### By V. June Collins

Now a FRIEND, just the other day,
Paused a bit when I heard him say,
"You know, you ROCK as you WALK?"
I smiled at him, 'n began to TALK.

You can check this out onto YOUR PAGE.
Has something to do with MY AGE.
I tend to LEAN each step 'n stride.
As each foot REVS for another ride.

YES, back 'n forth, like a mercury switch.
AT TIMES I stagger, lunge 'n sort-a pitch.
Hesitation Waltz? Be it forward or back.
Grip my toes to then stay on track.

An alternative choice, though quite great,
Might be golden years without GOLD PLATE.
Letting life pass by, reminiscing the wear,
While sittin', rockin', in old ROCKIN' CHAIR.

Or maybe six feet under? M-m-m- sort-a GRIM!
'Cause, we know not when we're nearing end.
To leave Old Earth, be a fond complaint.
Will not be easy, THAT SHE AIN'T!

Though Heaven's a grand PLACE TO BE!
Earthly green pastures very dear to me!
So I chose this route of WALK 'n ROCK.
It's all built in to my BOOTS 'n SOCK!

*This gives you a peek into another happening.*

## WHEELS TO DEAL
### By V. June Collins

Raised 'n showed Buckskin horses
Steadily, for nigh on to thirty years.
Raised 'n worked those personalities
With much happiness and some tears.

Most days not nearly long enough.
Some horses took turns, after dark.
One on night shift, that's for sure,
7 to 11, to make treasured mark.

With ground work 'n wet blankets,
He progressed, to make me proud.
Was 16 hands 'n quite a stretch.
Ladder needed, I tell you loud.

As my legs get shorter every year,
Need a side hill to get aboard.
Didn't tell horse this was my problem.
Might've unloaded me before moored.

Had many up's along the way.
Some slammed me a bit around.
Was still a great 'n happy life,
Far better than it may sound.

Three-wheelers came into existence.
Jerry, I'm sure, wished for one.
So he bought me one for Christmas.
Said it would be lots of fun.

I thought, it's just what I don't need
Though, to please, I'd learn to ride.
It was one cross-eyed actin' critter.
Made feelings somewhat hard to hide.

Photo By Jerry Collins

V. June on her wheel 'n deal 'n, three-wheeler.

No matter which way I'd try to go,
It very soon came plain to see
We're not communicating very much,
Was still contrary as it could be.

You see, I'm used to leggin' horses.
This thing's mind is like berserk!
When I legged it for a left turn,
It only 'sulled', with smile 'n smirk.

Instinctive habits I've learned for life,
They sure would have to be all undone
For this three-wheelin', balky varmint
Was always boundin' off, 'n on the run.

To make left turn, practiced weight shift
Onto floor board's outside rail.
This being just opposite, not natural,
When in the saddle, in front of tail.

Finally that day arrived. I made up my mind.
Said to Jerry,"You can have this ornery sloop.
By the time I've mastered all its know how,
My horse sense will have flown the coop."

So made a deal, right then 'n there
To trade to him for a tractor, small,
That would dig and cut the grasses,
Both scraggly and very tall.

Then I went on doing what comes naturally,
Though perhaps would be ridin' for a fall.
Can teach some old dogs a few new tricks
But it's much easier to chase the ball.

Photos By V. June Collins

While its hats off with the old
And back on with the new.
Brush knocks them off, to ground,
And horses, re-wear them, like shoe.

Photo By V. June Collins

Domino waiting impatiently in camp, for another days ride.

Photo By Jerry Collins

June on Domino, early in the morning, before the cold fog had burned off. On one of five Sheltowee, Trail rides in Kentucky, she and Jerry participated in.

*For five years, in the 1980's Jerry and I went on the Appaloosa Sheltowee Trail Ride in Kentucky, riding a hundred miles each year. A total distance of 500 miles. Sheltowee was the name the Indians gave Daniel Boone, meaning "big turtle."*

## DOMINO

### By V. June Collins

We rented horses for this ride.
In Kentucky, a few years back.
Mine, a four year old Appaloosa
Gelding, was a bit green, in fact.

He was flashy, black and white,
Who at times, had his way.
I noticed he kept lipping his bit
Much of the time as if in play.

We're asked pretty soon, to trot out,
I felt his lipping's, sudden clamp.
He had climbed into drivers seat
He thought, I should take a nap.

Wow! Right away I'm wide awake.
Realized he was cold-jawing, bit.
I yanked reins hard, right then left,
Tried to loosen-up clamp he had on it.

Scared, I jerked harder! Got rougher!
In wild effort, to loosen up his grip,
To hurt him enough, to get his attention,
Back 'n forth. Oh, just to pinch his lip.

We're then crashing over brush 'n rocks
Much like FIDO playfully carrying bone.
Standing in my stirrups, all determined
Still he's bounding straight ahead, alone.

This probably went on thirty times
Before I felt a tooth, slightly slip.
I poured on more coal, with brutal force,
Suddenly I feel his teeth, slip their grip.

Keen relief surged over and through me,
Like fresh breath, when all is gone.
Riding free wheeling, out of control,
Is no rider's planned-for song.

I've had horses run away with me,
When could guide some, but not stop.
But a horse clamped onto cheek piece,
Staight ahead, for sure, is all you got.

Horse's mind locks onto what he's doing.
On what's ahead, he just pulls the shade.
He'll run smack into tree, or over bluff,
With you, into danger, he'll quickly wade.

The feeling of doom soon descends.
A wreck in process, is building fast.
A horse so hell-bent on what he's doing
Can quickly crash, and burn your past.

I watched him closely, the rest of day.
Would feel him reach for bit's shank.
Which-ever side I felt this lipping,
I gave a hard jerk, 'n definite yank.

By day's end, he's getting my message
That this bit, was staying center field.
His mouth each time, getting more tender,
He needed to give me that bit, 'n yield.

Rode him 20 miles each day, for a week.
Also, each saddling he improved his walk.
Communications proved, rewarding
While I let him know, with talk.

I started getting more the feel of him
And he too, seemed to try and please.
The week wore on, without an incident
From some other colty sorts, of tease.

One cold morning, frost white upon ground,
And we're all going calmly along the trail,
We, probably about sixth in line, from front,
When he stopped like a glued down, snail.

Lowered his head, way-down, to investigate.
He was eyeballing, some strange sight.
Yellow jackets! Cold, barely able to fly,
Were just circling above ground, a might.

Their nest hole, right in the middle of trail.
Horses ahead, had rudely woke them up.
This green fellow, knew not, what they were,
He'd stopped, with nose, to whiff 'n snuff.

I kicked, whacked, yelled, to get him by.
Finally! One zapped him in the side!
Had near rodeo getting turned off of trail.
Jackets had started backing, into his hide.

On down trail, wheeled aside. I baled off.
Started swattin', these zingin', zappin' dudes.
He held real still, even leaned head over close,
Though my flapping gloves were quite rude.

I slapped his face all around his nose,
Into his flanks and on his belly, hard.
He never lost his cool, one little bit.
He'd gained faith, was saving of his lard.

Back there, they call these dudes, bees.
Are pretty darn big, for this definition.
Much bigger, than our brands of hornet...
And dispatching a meaner, disposition.

But next time heard yell, of more bees,
And I asked for dash, he hopped to!
Lessons are quickly learned, along trail
Daily ingrained, too become old-shoe.

He began also, to truly, walk right out.
Quit throwing an extra jig, in between.
By the end of week he was a pleasure.
No longer to old habits, did he lean.

"DOMINO," I rented another year and week.
We two, got along this time really fine.
While they do say it takes two to tango,
Would say that trip, was sure, sublime.

Yes, at times, when renting horses,
Have strong feeling, tables often turned.
Maybe should have, collected a salary
From what horses sometimes learned.

# WONT'S OF YOUTH

### By V. June Collins

Yearling calves, like teenagers,
Have need to roam and like to go,
Are headstrong when you're heading
Them back to herd, fast or slow.

They hyste their tails over backs,
In another direction pour on speed.
Work your old horse into big lather
Trying to prove their growing need.

You have vision of veal steaks now,
Wished-for and sizzling in the pan.
While each scatters much like quail
Just without any thoughts or plan.

Adverse, just opposite 'n contrary,
Runs in veins still not fully grown.
Can hope all will live through it,
'Cause this habit's not overblown.

Yet, on other hand, give thanks!
Without this reach, drive 'n roam,
Youths would all stay in their nests
'N never have a need to leave home.

# WAY IT IS
By V. June Collins

**RANCHERS 'n FARMERS earn their respectable class**
While feeding the nation under a large looking glass.
You might lift an eyebrow or just venture a snort.
It's really no picnic or a fine leisure resort.
**Environmentalists HARASS! Continually they chew.**
You're dammed if you don't 'n dammed if you do.
Watching greedy nation grow fat, as it feeds.
The basics ranchers have ARE BASICALLY NEEDS.
REMEMBER...
**While heifers into cows grow up through years,**
Old Bully Boys young ones, end up, many as steers.
Calves suck, sleep 'n play, fattening up fast.
Growing in bovine hides, off to market at last.
**After mares 'n stallions practice their thing,**
Foals, colts 'n fillies arrive in the spring.
Horses are cut. As GELDINGS, it quiets him down.
Sheep's, buck 'n ewes are lambing lambs, all around.
**When one in sheep band jumps high with a leap,**
Those that follow him act just like a SHEEP.
They'll mimic in line, right down to the letter.
Each follows the leader, tries repeating better.
Man has breeding stock, others stocking breeds.
While some raise ALFALFA, others grow WEEDS.
Always refining of lines. In just so many words,
As alter, cut 'n castrate each of their herds.
**Along same lines... If Criminals swiftly sent...**
These human abusers would become quickly bent.
Like truth in the Bible, plainly shown in text
**To answer with fear, THEY'D BE ALTERED NEXT!**
Yes, the end result still remains
Like both in the same class.
Change mind of these MALES
From FEMALES
To GRASS.

# OL' GIN BOB AND CORK

By V. June Collins

Ol' Gin Bob's headed back to pokey
For another long 'n lengthy stay.
Disturbing peace is frowned upon.
Time has come for him to pay.

Sobered him up to dry him out
Afore he's said he wanted Cure.
He took a long time deciding.
His mind's made up now, for sure.

Old Cork, his big ol' Airedale,
Would with us have to stay.
He'd be one mighty lonesome dog
For some months and by the day.

Wags his tail. Is man's best friend.
Really saying, "I still like home."
We sought his kind of reasons.
He just had reason not to roam.

Old Gin Bob said to tie him up,
"He won't need much attention,
Except you'll need to use a chain,
This I'd ought to mention.

Likes to keep teeth in shape
On the likes of any rope.
He will limber up his ivories
While giving himself some hope."

I just lead ol' Cork off a ways.
Longingly, he looked over shoulder.
Deep down inside I felt sorta sad,
Standing latched onto, tieing holder.

Had in my hand that chain for tie,
Though was a bit short on one end.
Now, to spy another link to tie onto
that would have just a bit of bend.

Ah! My eyes spied a hefty length.
Big derrick rope made of hemp.
It seemed to be just waiting.
Wouldn't need to spend a cent.

Managed to tie one burly end
To husky post with a bolen.
This idea surely now would work
Almost, as if it were stolen.

'Cause that other end had a ring
Woven neatly in, just right.
Would now, surely fill the bill
Was tough, could stand a fight.

So ambled on over with ol' Cork.
Had him up close, well in tow.
He started sizing up conditions
As if he was already on the know.

He would soon be moored here
In a strange and different place.
It seems he was accepting it
Almost meeting it, face to face.

He lapped a drink from the pan
Of the water cool and fresh.
Sat down beside it, heaved a sigh,
Tongue dangled like made of mesh.

He knew for sure, his freedom lie
At end of that there rope.
So he sidled on over casually
Gave a whiff, a sniff, 'n poke.

With his tongue, he sorta tasted.
Was quite familiar, but what size.
Would take a fair amount of time,
As feeling sure in his disguise.

I'm sure his plans had lighted,
Much like smoke is after spark.
He would not have long to wait
Before night turned into dark.

With patience and lots of space
Things never seemed so grim.
Ol' Cork had his very own plan
That had always worked for him.

He'd soon get down to business,
Would take just a bit more time.
Start grinding a groove around
With nary a sigh or whine.

We would see him mouthing
That old rope now and then.
Seemed slowly changed its shape.
Finally, one spot, clean and trim.

Still, he had a long way to go.
I thought, might even give it up.
That old rope was still holding
And he was not an ornery pup.

He'd woller it in mouth 'n rest
With his slobbers running drools.
Teeth made only little headway,
From his double set of tools.

Finally chawed darn thing through,
Just laying there on ground.
And slowly hysted himself back up
Without making a single sound.

He walked off slowly, just a ways
Quick like, into a gallop flew!
Headin' home that's for sure!
Rope and chain a boundin' too!

Hot-footin' it back to Gin Bob's
In the still of another night.
Guess if I'd bet, I'd a lost it,
For hadn't kept him in my sight.

Perhaps a bit of egg on my face
For must now his retrieving go.
To get that sly, old devil dog,
That put on his silent show.

He didn't know that Gin Bob
wouldn't be home now to feed.
That he'd get mighty hungry
When his belly got that need.

Without more doggy *vittles
To fill up his empty space,
Ol' Cork sure would be hungry
After all this homeward race.

So went 'n gathered up ol' Cork,
And to bring him back again.
For he'd escape or get loose,
Might be just where or when?

For anything that's chewable
Is sure, not long, too work.
So I started thinking of iron,
'N cable or bars that I could jerk.

Added on another piece of chain.
Disconnected that sad old rope.
I'd just nip his ideas in the bud.
Still feeling somewhat a dope.

When warned about keeping Cork,
That I just might need a jail.
I knew now, what ol' Cork meant,
By his wagging, friendly, tail.

For most laws that fit the average
Seems with him, will not hold.
He'll get loose when he can,
And he's milder than he's bold.

For not that he isn't thankful,
From feedings from this host.
Oft' times lately, however, he's
Been seen, CHAWIN' on the post.

*From the heat of the day my mind began to search for cooling memories. I read some short lines I had jotted down sometime in the past. Yes, it was strange to write a poem of winter on a hot day. My challenge!*

### SOUND BARRIER
### By V. June Collins

Snow in depths lay padded
Had a white foreboding stare.
Cold quiet of the morning
Put its hush upon the air.
I held my breath to listen.
Its hush felt close 'n near.
So free 'n easy was its quiet
Near soundless, as is fear.

A peaceful slumber, welcomed,
Among snows piled on ground.
Morning's voice echoed, quiet,
My ears reaching for a sound.
Yes, wagon sounds, far muffled.
Wagon-jangles softly lost.
Each snow flake oiled and padded.
Distant silence, quiet, tossed.

Wind desperate from all its fury
Now lay licking of its wounds.
Bruised and beat in exhaustion
Softly whispered silent tunes
Winds lay sleeping in the clouds
And down in depths, not yet awake.
Winds, like some wild demon,
A tomorrow's blizzard makes.

*Recollections from yester-years. If you were lucky enough to also have plumbing in the house, so be it. The two-holer still had its attraction, especially when extra help or company arrived.*

## OLD PINCH BOTTOM

By V. June Collins

In Bogus country, up Lemos way,
They had a two-holer with a name.
She was called, Old Pinch Bottom,
Which was her claim to fame.

*Previously Published:1992 Collected Works of Siskiyou--Coyote Publishing; In 1999, Songs of the Siskiyou's-- Living Gold Press*

Old Pinch Bottom was a stinker.
She had a swingin' squeaky door.
Customers waited sometimes in line
To ply their usual chore.

You'd hear a loud yip! and echo
In the quiet still of day or night.
Some came back out bashful, quiet.
Others cussin' and on the fight.

No one for long escaped her.
She was silent like a thief.
Also knew, in time, you'd visit.
If not for welfare, for relief.

Each time the dread built up.
Your trips were some delayed.
Memories kept you waiting,
As oft' times your mind replayed.

Sure, you'd carefully try to miss
That crack, waiting on the seat.
Its grab felt like a bear trap.
Was both split and tried to meet.

You'd think you had it mastered.
For at times, all seemed well.
'Til Old Pinch Bottom, with revenge,
Raised your voice into a yell!

The rest of time she was ignored.
At least, no one tried to fix.
With a smirk, waited for strangers.
Was almost like playing tricks.

While another unsuspecting victim came
To sit leisurely upon the throne,
The waiting silence was most deafening.
Never a bit of sympathy was shown.

Old Pinch Bottom left a deep impression
That might resemble, sometimes, a fit!
Your mind told you, "You must stand up."
While your bottom said... TO SIT!

OFF BALANCE

By V. June Collins

With years of riding horses
Ever so often hit the dirt.
Sometimes from using spurs
When needed a bat or quirt.

Just get caught off balance
To the point of no return.
Yes, may pull some leather,
Or lose stirrup, with concern.

Many say, "Got bucked off!"
From here, I just might scoff.
I've fell off many more times
Than did ever get bucked off.

Photo By V. June Collins.
Then some days it rains on the trail.

Photo By V. June Collins

Little North Fork, Salmon River. This picture is taken from the Forks of The Salmon bridge. The Salmon River is frozen over, showing a frozen whirlpool in motion. One of the latter places to freeze. The whirlpool water beneath, continues to circle, releasing a circle of ice as the temperature rises. The center section, is thawed and spinning, where only a short time before it had been frozen in place. Probably it will freeze at night, if temperatures again drop.

## SALMON RIVER

By V. June Collins

The North and South fork both,
Elbow their way among the rocks.
Little Northfork pushes, swiftly,
Its cold water above your hocks.

Down stream it wildly tumbles
Still writhing where it fell.
Later saunters like sleeping.
Needs to meander for a spell.

At The Forks of Salmon Bridge
Waters from its mountains meet.
Our eyes beholden to this sight
Of frosted flakes, in icy sheet.

Cold fingers reach across water.
Each night it gains more space.
Waters soon become imprisoned
Clasped beneath its cold embrace.

Winter sun but rarely touches
Freezing cold in great supply.
Ice crowds every shoreline,
Shivers beneath its sullen sky.

We watched Ma Nature's artwork.
Before eyes, it began to thaw.
Drops trickle, restless downward,
From dripping winter's icy jaw.

Melting ice, tickled stirring,
Around the whirlpool's glassy eye.
Warmer waters  beneath circle,
Carved free, to spin on high.

Like skating nymphs out playing
Started circling round 'n round.
Old river rares back into motion.
Again hear, her gurgling sound.

Stan Cooley roping on "Brownie," at the home ranch in Shasta Valley, near Agar

Stan at the ranch, breaking foal, "Priss" to lead, 2002.

Photos By Betty Cooley

These Mexican steers, were sure in luck.

*Stan Cooley, a long time Shasta Valley rancher, and cowboy, told me this story shortly after its happening, forty years ago. With a smile of understanding, again, it here surfaces.*

## STAN'S STONE BOATIN' STEER

By V. June Collins

A train was headin' up the SISKIYOUS
Soon found it had run amuck.
With a box car full of dogies.
MEXICAN STEERS, were now in luck.

They scattered off into the hills.
FREEDOM was within their reach.
In was a cold kind of winter weather,
Not some sunny, southern beach.

Friend, STAN COOLEY and his CRONIES,
Started rounding up each steer.
And in this wild, smart, wily bunch
Were many cunning, like a deer.

THEIR MEMORY STAYS OUTSTANDING
Like a hole remembered in a fence.
Waiting until their need arises,
Then their radar tracks don't mince.

HIDE 'n SEEK became their game.
Had to dislodge singly, every stray.
Felt at times they'd been greased,
So quickly they'd get away.

They finally got them to the ranch,
Out near AGER, where they would stay.
This would be their home for awhile,
Be it a year, a month, or a day.

Appetites are GOOD, just about content,
Except for one, that's ailing some.
Most were gladly munching chow.
Still, Ol' Laggard wouldn't come.

That Ol' steer, sure now, was sick.
To the barn, we'd just have to bring.
Stan hitched onto, old *stone boat.
Would drag in that DING-A-LING.

***Stone Boat**: *is a wooden sled, dragged by a team of horses or tractor. It's built husky, with its top about twelve to fifteen inches from ground. Its name is derived from its original use, of loading rocks onto, when clearing fields*

In desperation, steer was loaded on
MUCH LIKE DISHWATER, FROM A PAN.
A lifeless sort of lump, there lay,
Waiting for the wish of man.

He was dragged on inside, corral
And CLOSED BEHIND him, the GATE.
Ol' Steer lay aboard much, uncaring,
Was just waiting for his fate.

POKED A FEW NEEDLES IN HIS HIDE.
That get well serum, did the job!
He started in, to acting perky,
From that wad of hair 'n glob.

STAN forked hay quite near his head.
And put some water within reach.
Ol' steer thought it was his pulpit.
IF A PREACHER, HE WOULD PREACH.

Each day, Ol'steer, got a little better.
Not far from STONE BOAT, did he roam.
Feedin' time, he'd climb back aboard.
Showed appreciation for his throne.

These groceries sure did come easy.
All most like heaven, doing well.
It sure beats rangin' wild, BY THUNDER!
He thinks,"He'll just stick around a spell."

Yes, he's one smart BOVINE HOMBRE.
He was plum clever, from the start.
When he got his hay served up, on a platter,
A SPECIAL, STONE BOAT, KIND OF CART!

# BALING WIRE

By V. June Collins

Baling Wire, Old Twine's brother,
Lived life scattered, much the same.
A necessity on both ranch and farm.
Grudgingly, we just call its name.

Follows each row out in field.
Grabs 'n wraps hay up within.
It's hard to find a place today
Old Baling Wire hasn't been.

Repairs are temporary permanent.
Sure seems to be quite the mix.
A glue that holds all together
Is one quick binder and a fix.

Splices fences, wires up gates.
Find its uses there, are many.
For sure when things break down,
Worth more than a pretty penny.

Photo by V. June Collins

A second life given these old mowing machine blades. Here barring windows on old building.

Photo By V. June Collins

*Baling Twine stack that interestingly grows with age along the highway near Herlong, California, and adds a bright spot to the scenery. Knowing that many bovine bellies received some warmth from hay, during the cold winter, from these binders*

## BALING TWINE

By V. June Collins

From a large baling twine pile,
Come even more fix-all, repair.
Holds scads of things together
Both super fine, to middlin fair.

Often, temporary permanent
But sure will last a long time.
While wait for new, might be
Far longer, than this rhyme.

Red color, quite eye catching
Both in spring and on the snow.
Sometimes along in late winter,
Like sprouts, seems near to grow.

Some drivers pass without a glance.
Its view also, known to stop cars.
It might take on look of a monster,
Beamed down from planet Mars.

Baling Twine lays in deaths struggle
Lying there exhausted in a heap.
Its battle had raged on for months.
Seems slung down, into sad defeat.

Chunks and pieces sagging laxly
Upon both sage and on the fence.
Limp, breathless, quiet still, lifeless,
What future monument will commence.

Old Baling Twine's not a slouch.
For it too, has many other uses.
'Tis braided, twisted, fashioned,
Twirled by many kids, in nooses.

Is seen wound into, giant balls,
For eye to marvel at and view.
Have not yet, added vitamins 'n flavor
For old bossy to gum and chew."

I know when viewing this memento
Empty truck had stopped at gate.
They'd thrown off remaining ties,
While old motor champed, in wait.

Would later reload, for next morning.
When again, cattle hungry and all cold.
This regular chore would repeat itself
As is well built, into rancher's mold.

*Written after reading a joke in The Reminisce Magazine in 1995, that tickled my funny-bone.*

## POLITICIAN'S MISTAKE
### By V. June Collins

Plane droned steadily onward
Through night and into dawn.
Its three passengers, by turn,
Gave some sighs and a yawn.

When cabin door flew open wide
And PILOT strode in, proud.
He said, "I must inform you."
(His voice was becoming loud.)

"I'm sorry to tell you this,
but she's almost out of gas.
Plane will soon be leaving us
And be heading down to grass."

"There are only three parachutes
And this one I must take.
You see, I'm scheduled in again
On another flight must make."

With flourish, hopped out the door.
Disappeared quickly out of sight.
Heard engine cough and sputter,
Tolling near-end of this flight.

POLITICIAN jumped to his feet.
Pulled his hat down real tight.
Made a wild dash for the door
Said, "Truthfully it's my right."

In an instant he disappeared
From that doorway like a breeze
Leaving PREACHER and the STUDENT
Both feeling a bit ill at ease.

The PREACHER and the STUDENT,
Quite alone, and looking grim.
PREACHER thought, "My life's been
good. I'll give that chute to him."

He lowered head and closed his eyes,
Shoulders looked somewhat slumped.
Student yelled! "We got Two Chutes!
POLITICIAN in my backpack, JUMPED."

*Jerry and I were driving back home from Medford, Oregon, in January of 1996 when the conversation of second childhood came up. I told Jerry this was my thinking and he laughed and said, "Why don't you write a poem about it?" By the time we arrived home my rough version was in the pages of my note book which I often carry with me, to jot down thoughts.*


## SECOND CHILDHOOD

By V. June Collins

Have you ever taken time to wonder
Just what time in your lives...
That you might become acquainted
With Second childhood as it arrives?

I think I've found an answer,
At least, where it got its name.
For when you'r in Second Childhood,
Don't have to take much blame.

When we're young, as little children,
Could hardly wait, until grown up.
Would brag about how old we were
Though pretty much still a pup.

Finally middle age grabbed us,
Age was hidden, a secret be.
It became no one else's business.
'Twas a fact most plain to see.

Life drifts on by, through many years,
Before Second Childhood comes to pass.
Then we see who has reached that goal,
Among bearded men, and wrinkled lass.

Those sounds of bragging, again, start up.
And hear, "Can you guess, how old am I?"
As reply follows, "Sure don't look that old!"
Causes a grin to spread, into happy sigh.

Age starts in attacking, all conversations
Seems sounds so good! On every page!
SECOND CHILDHOOD- has been reached...
**When again, start bragging of your age.**

I just thank my lucky stars, to be alive
For many cards dealt out, most kind.
And have been allowed to live, so long...
Intact, with some **retroactive** mind.

*The night of January 14, 1996, I had a vivid dream that was still harassing me next morning. After breakfast I was compelled to put it into verse.*

   DREAMS

By V. June Collins

Jerry and I walked down a long hall.
Before leaving, had need to stop.
I dodged into the ladies' room,
With a few quick steps, and hop.

Room was strange, I quite surprised,
Was not the cubical that I sought.
A great big, open, spacious room.
My journey now seemed fraught.

This room was wall-to-wall and dotted
With many little round tufted stools
Where many familiar ladies sat visiting.
Some were crocheting fast, like fools.

I walked about, looked and examined,
Like toad stools, all looked the same.
It was sometime before I discovered...
Only one, had different lid and chain.

It still looked so very strange to me,
But was sure plain, that it must be.
What I thought I was looking for,
In prayer, and almost bended knee.

There in pleasure I quickly sat down
While my eyes sharply, looked aside.
Was sitting next to big glass window,
Out in plain sight... I nearly cried.

Friends started coming by to chat.
Pat Martin sat down for a visit too.
Seemed no one felt my predicament.
Was like no one else even knew.

My burden became much heavier,
Like some big weight upon my chest.
No one, seemed one bit, to notice.
Why, I was sitting there, like rest.

They talked and passed time of day.
My feelings became most galled.
Suddenly, I seemed to be out in street,
Men and women stopped, and called.

I was caught up in this traffic
With little chance for my reprieve.
While I sat there in embarrassment,
I felt I could neither stay nor leave.

I couldn't' go, I couldn't stay,
If I stood up, they would know.
For was not a tufted stool I sat on.
Its strange lid and chain would show.

But finally, real miracle happened.
My worries were turned to peace.
By an alarm clock, I was awakened.
WILL WONDERS NEVER CEASE!

Photos By V. June Collins
Nine big State Highway signs on I-5 over the Siskiyous, on North side, warn travelers and truckers to watch for runaway ramps.

*We often travel over the Mountains of Siskiyou in Northern California where nine big State Highway,* ***"Runaway****  Truck Ramp" signs get your attention, each time as they warn travelers to watch for* ***runaway ramps.***
*This for years has caused much thought and wonderment. Surely they were meant to be* ***"Truck****, Runaway Ramps." After years of contradictory feelings, on our way to the coast, July 11, 1995, I finally felt compelled to write:*

### FLIGHT OF RUNAWAY TRUCK RAMP

By V. June Collins

Have you been over the Siskiyous lately?
See RUNAWAY TRUCK RAMPS as you pass?
This sure, will almost blow your mind,
And even make you step on the gas.

Signs - RUNAWAY, TRUCK RAMP!
Shout loud and clear, along the way.
Might Ramps, just up and skidaddle?
'Cause, that's what signs plainly say.

Its sure will be, quite unnerving,
As careening down off steep slope,
To not find any safe havens, waiting.
Instead, are off somewhere, on a lope.

Those truckers, over the Siskiyous
Sure do, have need to stay alert.
For when brakes start getting hot
'It's with death, they're asked to flirt.

'CAUSE,
Up in North State, we too, have Big Foot,
And Shasta Lamarians, out on prowl.
Siskiyou's sly cavorting, TRUCK RAMPS
Like packs of Coyotes, will yip 'n howl.

Have runaway horses, runaway teams,
And runaway box cars, on the track.
Where it seems, all heck breaks loose
Before someone takes up the slack.

Now RUNAWAY TRUCK RAMPS joined list.
It is rather confusing to say the least.
When we see a TRUCK RAMP, RUN AWAY
Would have to class it as a beast.

One gets that wild, scary, sort of vision
Big Runaway TRUCK RAMPS, in flight.
Quickly dodges to disappear in mist...
Most like the day does, into night.

Playing hide and seek with truckers,
Before dodging suddenly, off the road.
Without leaving any sign or inkling...
As to where to find a clue, or code.

Ramps meant to slow down demon trucks
Into one big, lassoed, sort of stop.
Where if wheels brake free, start racing
From down off, the high mountain top.

It is one life-line, most reassuring,
Placed below summit, for safety sake.
There, trucks looking for place to stop
Won't find a gosh-darned, sort of fake.

If signs read, TRUCK, RUNAWAY RAMP
Guess it would just seem more clear.
So wouldn't feel left, all in a quandry,
Coming off down highway, as we steer.

To be, in place and waiting there.
Not off somewhere else, galavanting
Leaving us and truckers in dispair.

We want to see them, each and every time,
Over that familiar old hill, we've drove.
Ramps parked, in place and waiting...
Stashed, just like haven in a cove.

It's just plain, good old, human nature
To start looking for stable place to land.
Because whenever we get into trouble...
Oft' times, land up, where not planned.

# WILLS, WILES AND WON'T

By V. June Collins

Almost as if wired and feeling sparks,
Feet bounding high from each track
Young calf's tail, like electric charged
Is hysted, scared, above his back.

Don't think he's about to be corraled.
He'll squirt into another direction seek.
I feel like a magnet of opposite pole
When his distance, he's allowed to keep.

He's headed for that brushy hillside.
Will try to scratch me from his mind.
Figures there, he will get upper hand
When I'm then forced to seek and find.

Yes, I'm still gaining on the bugger.
Finally we're almost in dead heat.
Yet, it might not be so very long
Before might up and admit defeat.

Before old horse is wore to frazzle,
Might be time we should ride away.
Let him play his hard-to-get game.
Just leave him there, like stray.

Go back and find his bawling mamma.
Ease her up hill to maverick calf.
Give him time to chow-down a bit.
Might cut this chore about in half.

While together, they might come slowly,
Not much pushing if you please.
Just a little bit more patience
With some time, too slowly ease.

If they think going is their idea
And I don't have much need to care,
We'll probably get them to the bottom
All together, back as a pair.

Yes, we can lead our horse to water
Though sure can't make him drink.
So what makes us think we are boss
If old cow 'n calf are on the think?

# PARTS AND PIECES

## By V. June Collins

The palm in your hand is not a tree
But has lines like trails beneath.
Life lines, 'tis said to surely be
Whether long length or quite brief.

We have corns on toes, ears on head,
Where ears of corn don't grow.
Eardrums you don't want to beat,
Even if putting on quite a show.

On bridge of nose nostrils are crossed
Sometimes with cold, runs like a river.
Your eyes may cross at sight of it all,
If you imbibe, will affect your liver.

A cap on your knee is sure not a hat
Yet, still covers your knee joint well.
Just wait, 'til you get some older,
A different limping story may tell.

Both shoulder blades are flat and sharp.
With them, can't cut or trim your hair.
While calf on leg, not heard to bawl,
Takes off on a run, with wear and tear.

Nails on fingers if driven with hammer,
Have a result quite different indeed.
May just go squash, you holler and yell,
While the red drops blister and bleed.

Nap of neck still not quite asleep
Where crick in neck, wished to be.
Hump in your back follows you about
Like your shadow, it's plain to see.

Ball on your foot, sure not a game
But plays an active role and part.
When you've slid to a sliding stop
Or when heading quickly off on start.

When old spur on heel is still ouchy,
Right where you've so often appealed.
Guess still have much time to wonder
Why heel on my foot not healed?

Depression beneath shoulder and arm
Is where armpits are said to be.
While plum and cherry each have a pit,
A pitfall usually not easy to see.

Roots of hair not sprouting growth
On top of balding, bare head and pate.
Ancestors' roots can take some blame.
Heredity's rooted, in acts of fate.

Prints on fingers, though hard to read,
Make a statement that's truly a fact.
Each one of us is proven different,
No matter how much the same we act.

If the bend of your knee not a route
Along the river or winding trail,
Why is battlefield of "Wounded Knee,"
Way out where histories prevail?

Really, the truth of the matter remains,
Hope head on my shoulders stays sound.
Still, a time when I was found wailing,
Poor knees had some let me down.

Life's been a good one, without any doubt,
On its path like strong rudder and sail.
Finally decided needed route of repair,
When bend in my trail began to fail.

If knob on my knee could open the door
So as to grease those old joints up well,
There might just be more to this story,
Perhaps much more, than I'm able to tell.

Photos by V. June Collins
Caught between listening sessions at Stockman Hotel room. Hats and boots catching a bit of rest, too, during one of our four and five day stays in Elko, Nevada. June Severns has also attended a number of these annual entertainments with the Collins.' A habit we look forward to seeing.

V. June again bound for Elko, Nevada, for the fourteenth year, to hear the annual, incredible, non-stop Cowboy Poetry and Music entertainment. Held the last week of January into February each year.

The population swells to more than 8000 persons during this annual event.

Enthusiasts arrive from all over the 50 States as well as Canada, Australia, Ireland, and Mexico, plus other Countries and far away places, everyone comes to hear poetry of Life the experiences, Old Classics, and Western Heritage happenings, unraveled into their ears from many talented Authors and Reciters.

Some of these performances are available to view on the Web.--Try it! You might like it!

Photo By Jerry Collins

www.westfolk.org/gathering.html

# MILEAGE CHECK

By V. June Collins

Yes, I have laugh lines and crowfeet
Plainly etched upon my face.
At times, feel could do without
But to ponder, would be a waste.

I'm told they're lines of character
Just a map of likely codes
That clutter up smooth, clear skin
With lines that resemble roads.

Cover distance that I've traveled
Like mile posts, recording miles.
Added on fuel it took, to here arrive
Required both scowls and smiles.

Life has been a good one, special,
Filled in a variety of clouds and sun.
Along way, each day was registered.
I've earned each and every one.

Sometimes, still feel I'm youthful
Until the mirror shakes its head.
Saying, Sister, you're nearly ancient
Oft' times, can hardly get out of bed.

You take each step, one at a time,
And I almost never see you run.
I think you'd better look again,
You're sure not thirty-one!

*This poem brought to pass from a well liked work boot that has served men and women for many years. I often shudder on seeing its misuse, by those thinking they are pure WESTERN -- A new generation without knowledge of this boot's evil strength when used for another purpose other than what it was intended.*

## PACKERS, BROGANS AND LACERS
(work boots)
By V. June Collins

When young and first began riding horses
It was strictly bare-back all the way.
Parents knew we'd often fall off
And would not be hung up in our play.

Our balance improved by trial and error.
Their worries for sure were much less.
We'd get back on and soon try again.
Episodes here learned, I will confess.

Old horse chosen was somewhat ancient.
His cow-smarts much exceeded ours.
We soon learned from his knowledge
Absorbed like quiet rain from showers.

Usually he got us where we needed to be
Which made us feel real good, inside.
Old horse taught us a great big lot
On his daily, often schooling, ride.

Our first stirrups had leather covers.
Attached to saddle called our own.
Assured, small feet not slip through.
Pride gladly rode, as safety shown.

Finally day came for very own horse.
Special joy lasted near on forever.
Practiced what old horse taught us.
Tried to make new horse be as clever.

For that day might come when he, too,
Would be someone else's teacher.
'Cause honest horses are in demand.
All want this dependable feature.

Western boots, been around since 1880
Still they are as necessary as can be.
Especially, upside down from old saddle.
Letting whole body swing wild and free.

Western boots have a need and purpose
When bucked off and hung up in a storm.
A safety valve, might work quite handy.
Foot slides out while alive and warm.

BROGAN, a work boot, is on stampede, running
Toward ready made suicide and dude's strife.
Does O S H A * ride herd for safety sake?
Are Lacers just waiting to take your life?

Young things, think they're really WESTERN
In many colors, worn by rank and file.
LACERS, PACKERS, BROGAN WORK BOOTS
Have now become the dumbest style.

They sure weren't built to sit a horse,
Especially ones that shy, buck and such,
'Cause when old stirrup grabs a hold, hard,
Like a bear trap, she'll keep in touch.

Should fancy PACKER decide to stay put
In a stirrup, for which it was not made,
Hope you have your gun loaded, and ready,
For in deep trouble you're bound to wade.

Life may depend on you cocking hammer,
Shooting old horse fast, here and now.
Head's plum soft when wearing PACKERS.
Old horse, next, will use it for a plow.

He'll bang your head from side to side.
Each crack and pop will speed him on.
'Tis an extended, helpless way to die.
Life ebbs slowly, before senses gone.

Just think again, when wearing PACKERS.
Keep feet somewhat close to the ground.
They're sure built for wear and workin',
Not Western, or riding to the hounds.

Cause long after you are dead and gone
Loved ones again, wipe tears and cry.
PACKERS weren't meant for riding horses.
Don't let some new style, blind your eye.

* OSHA:
Occupational Safety
and Health Act

## OTHER BOOT REASONS

### By V. June Collins

Loggers add corks to their stogy boots
Like porcupine quills into sturdy soles.
Latches feet down each step 'n stride
And to roll logs with prod and poles.

Hard toes were added for safety sake
Boy! Did it ever protect their toes.
Sturdy built wear was now built-in
While relieving some whys and woes.

Farmers and workers wore old brogans
Strongly laced, gave them strength.
Can bet, hikers liked what they saw.
High tops were added to their length.

World War I and II was then the fad
Officers, motorcycle riders all use,
Air-Force also took on this look
While was in place quickly lit a fuse.

They then came near up to their knees.
Were thought looked most fitting too.
Later Red Setter's sponge soles arrived.
Hunters quickly sought this special shoe.

Yes, fads have always been much around
Where a style hurts not another soul.
Only labeled today as WESTERN WEAR
Sure does not set well within my bowl.

*Christmas Eve 1996. We had finished eating supper. I lingered, still sitting at table. Jerry had gone into watch TV. The real Night Before Christmas story came to mind. I dismissed it. Again, I found I was repeating it in silence. Thoughts occurred... Tonight was another Night Before Christmas, at our house. A strange quiet abounded. It was our first year to have no children, grandchildren, or Great-Grands in abundance. We were alone until tomorrow noon. My thoughts emerged into activity. Words took shape, soon fell into place behind my pencil, within the hour arrived.*

## NIGHT BEFORE CHRISTMAS

By V. June Collins

**Was The Night before Christmas**
Home of old dog, cats, and mouse.
Cat soundly was sleeping, while
Old dog, Biscuit, guarded the house.
**Santa came back from the chimney.**
Found it much to small to go down.
Hurriedly, he slid off the rooftop,
With another quick hop, and a bound.
**Now Santa needed to walk bent over**
From weight piled onto his back.
Want lists bulged in anticipation,
Wrapped boxes stuck out of his sack.
**His sleigh bells jangled so softly,**
Squeeky foot steps echoed, a bit loud.
Deep snows lay softly drifted,
Foot prints shown, widely plowed.
**Santa gathered his wits, up, about him,**
And slipped quietly, up to the door.
He turned the knob, ever so gently,
When out of his grasp, it was tore.
**Seems winter's gusty, cold breeze**
Had turned quickly, into a blast.
Violently, jerked door, wide open,
And wrenched it, right out of his clasp.

**Toys were everywhere, scattered.**
Things looked a mess, that's for sure.
Old Santa picked himself up slowly
From where he lay in heap on the floor.
**Wild clatter, really, disturbed old Biscuit.**
While shadows, had given him a scare.
Events happened fast, thereafter.
Will make an attempt, to here share
**As dark shadow crossed the window,**
And crept silently up, toward door.
Old Biscuit, became most vigilant,
He bounded, straight up from the floor.
**He managed barely, to stay upright**
On throw-rug, placed to catch drip.
He quickly was airborne, into flight
On a dog-gone, runaway, rug trip

**On past Santa, he sailed like a vision,**
That old dog, riding fast. on a rug.
Into storm,clouds he quickly disappeared.
Santa, just gave his shoulders a shrug.
**Santa still had a long ways to travel.**
Somewhere between and betwixed.
He managed to leave off their gifts
Though stirred, and a little bit mixed.
**Had been a long time since he'd eaten.**
He felt hungry, started looking around.
Spied a large plate of fresh cookies,
And large glass of milk to gulp down.
**He sat down on chair, and pondered.**
For  a little while, only, could he rest.
This is where old Biscuit caught him.
But maybe, you have already guessed.
**Aloft, Old Biscuit was quite bedazzled,**
His next thought was how to get down.
Rug seemed to have mind, all its own,
As it let him view, all lights, of the town.

**Discovered he could change his direction,**
By just wagging his tail to and fro.
In excitement he wagged round and round,
While old rug made two loops, in a row.
**He crouched, leaned, and he squatted,**
He began circling downward to earth.
Trying to slow down, that rollicking rug,
To again land, at the place of his birth.
**Finally he sat down, tucked his tail under.**
That flapping contraption, eased to stop.
Floating like leaf, down to his doorway,
Barking loud, as bounded off from its top.

**Door still left open, a-jar waiting,**
Biscuit's return came sudden, and swift.
Like cyclone, he dashed through doorway,
Snow sprayed ahead of him, out of a drift.
**Old Santa, fairly flew out that door.**
Of course was in opposite direction.
It was for sure, not long, did he tarry
Nor take a view of his moving reflection.
**When he hit that wide open doorway**
He too, disappeared, fast into the night
For he's atop that very same old rug,
And launched him quickly, off into flight.

**Now you won't see Santa so often,**
Out in the snow, riding his sleigh,
For he has found, this flying old rug
Sure can make, a quick get-away.
**Santa just keeps on riding, his old carpet.**
While his reindeer, get a good rest.
Christmas greeting he'll keep on sending,
From The East, And Out Of The West.

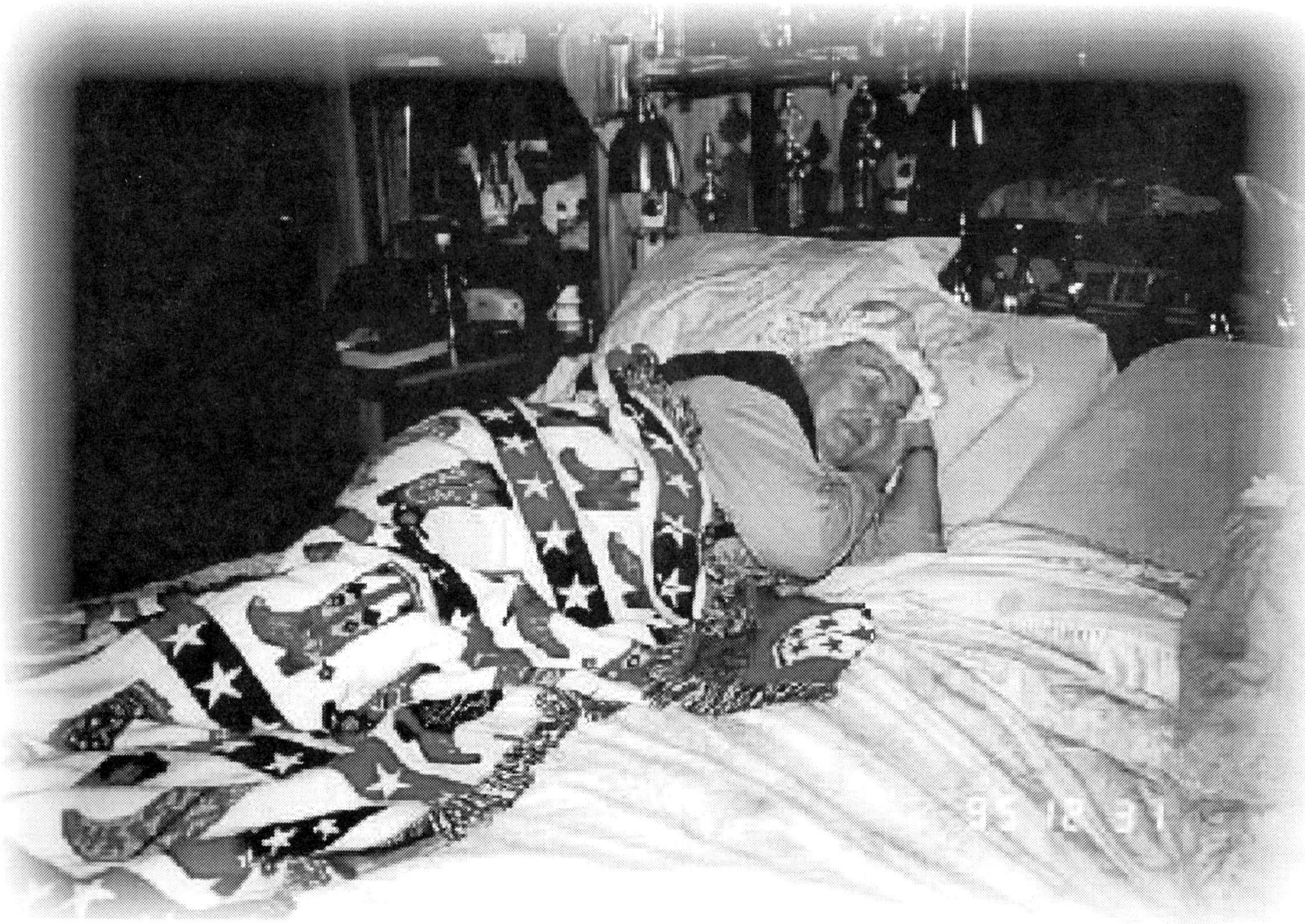

## AFTER CHRISTMAS

Photo By Jerry Collins

By V. June Collins

Yes wrappings all disposed of,
Left narry a crinkle of sound.
Christmas rush had subsided,
Felt its soft quiet abound.

Its a few days after Christmas
Right here in the house,
Nana's caught snoozing in
Jeans, sweatshirt and blouse.

She'd added her vest, so as
To be, snuggled down warm.
For on outside, snowflakes
Blew about in the storm.

She was nestled down com-fy
With her cap on her head,
Under a cozy soft blanket,
On her oversized bed.

When an ogre appeared
With camera in hand
His flash bulbs a flashin'.
Oh, man... Oh, man!

Quickly nap was here ended
From a head full of dreams,
While here ends this story.
Just vamoosed! It seems.

# WHAT AGE
(Watt-age)
## By V. June Collins

Now this had allowed, my mind to wander
Back into my early days of youth.
How being young had warped my thinking
Seems had strayed, off, from the truth.

Was eight or so, most nearly grown
I thought 30 years to be really old.
When clock turned to a full thirteen,
And 40... somehow, was nearing cold.

At 50... One foot was in grave, for sure.
Hardly thought of those thereafter.
Yet, when I reached that plateau of 65,
Seem was reading another chapter.

While clambering over rocks of time,
Still was having loads of fun.
Could see new handwriting on the wall.
Why, 70... Appeared quite young.

80... not near the obstacle, I surmised.
Could most see 90...merge in view.
Though 100... seems quite a ways away,
Sure now, with luck, may get there too.

Have reached an age, of how old I am,
Seems now, really not much to matter.
'Cause some days am younger than I feel,
While other days, just bang and clatter.

Discovered, all ages, have much to offer
And hope my mind upstairs, stays intact.
In gear, continue to loap along my trail,
Swingin' my rope, and gather up slack.

*What's in a name.* I too, researched a number of different historical issues, of Siskiyou County, and found different opinions. I called Cline Soule, who still ranches in Tailholt area. Both he and sister, Bernice Meamber, were born in Tailholt. Soule said, "His mother told him, cattle were driven from Butte Valley to Tailholt, in Shasta Valley fairly regularly, in early times. One morning while some cattle were being worked there, they were having trouble catching one, old cow, when someone suggested they use a tailhold on her, which they did with success. She thought this was why, Tailholt had gotten its name.

Now presume at that time, the person which made this tailhold suggestion, either had the know how, or was a Mexican Vaquero. One, who could quickly dump a running bovine, with a applied tailhold. If so, this could very well be the true reason for **Tailhold** name. Had this area become known for this kind of control method, it also, like many American names, quickly corrupted from Tailhold, to Tailholt.

I have watched Mexican Vacqueros, horse back in Mexico, dump steers at a full gallop, time after time. The rider catches up to a running steer, rides along beside (somewhat similarly to bull dogging), instead of reaching for horn he grabs the tailhold, as they go by. He throws his stirrup and leg around and over the tailhold, and down goes, the bovine, almost as if rolled in own hide. A helper can grab its horns, with his knee into its neck, and twist nose up and back. Animal can be branded or tied, before the shock wears off. It does have a tendency to take some of the starch out of, a most determined critter!

**Tailholt Mailboxes Of Shasta Valley -- Tilt An Ear And Listen.**  Photo By Jerry Collins

## TAILHOLT, MAIL BOXES

By V. June Collins

Back in past, old town of TAILHOLT stood,
Bustling along, with its horse and wagon gait.
Into those 1880's was quite the busy place,
Where today, only mailboxes stand in wait.

Then had two stores with supplies to sell,
Plus two saloons, and a harness shop.
Had a meat market and a slaughter house
Both a baseball park and race track, stop.

Though not etched in our memories, today
We know, by those words passed down.
When see patient mailboxes, like gathering,
Marking time, in absences of their town.

Mail Boxes, perched upon posts and plank,
In a row, their sizes differ and vary some.
Quiet Mail Boxes, with built in patience,
Yet, all appear anxious for the mail to come.

They always seem pleased, to see the mail man.
He appears to feed, before he drives away.
What has more patience, than an old mail box
With its long waits, for visits, twice each day?

Mailman sometimes scurries as he stuffs,
Like each box, almost had a hungry mouth.
Grouped, clustered, stand in utter silence,
Together, through rain, sun and drought.

Awaiting letters, flyers and package arrivals.
Boxes then settles down for another wait.
Sometimes only for a few short minutes...
Other times might be, just ever so late.

Owners find time, finally, to check boxes,
Still, all this time, patiently, waiting you see.
Feel warm glance, when a letter is opened...
Like friend's distant smile, and fond Tee-Hee!

Often times of late, these past few years,
Junk mail, caused some frowns, to ponder.
Whether should pack it on back to the house,
Or maybe ought to toss high, into yonder.

Each rancher, soon drives back away.
And somber faced boxes, look content.
Sitting on roosts, like a family, all together,
Awaiting those messages, from where ever sent.

# NEW COW'S REPUTATION

## By V. June Collins

Grandma, Coe bought a neighbor's cow,
Horseback, Sister and I, drove her home.
We thought she came all by herself, but
Soon found, she did not come alone.

    Was asked to go fetch a bucket,
      For this cow had need of drain.
      Must relieve old bossy, pronto!
      'Cause, "She sure, must be in pain."

Being low man, on totem pole
Was elected to milk her dry.
So, upon stool with head in flank,
Squirts of milk into bucket, fly.

    Pail nearly full, I brought to kitchen,
      After a bit of time had past.
      Coe was pleased! Cow, good milker!
      I was thanked for my needed task.

I sat down on chair in the lamplight
Supper's preparation, sizzling high.
My head kept itching, for no good reason.
I finally complained and heaved a sigh.

    Mom said, "Come here!" "Closer to light.
    Let me have a good look and see."
    Heard in another breath, "You're lousy!"
    "Cow lice!" "You're as lousy, as can be!"

Mom fetched the lard pail to the counter
With her hand, scooped out a splat.
Plopped it atop my head and worked it in.
This changed these crawlies, traveling map.

I had to sit there, for about a half hour
Just to be sure, to do, those babies in.
With pans & pans of soapy warm water
Ended up refurbished, beginning to end.

This was before hot water came in faucets
Water then came from pump, by the pail.
And grease had a way of clinging on...
Much as fastened on, by tack and nail.

I would soap and my mom would rinse,
Slowly, we gained on grease and critters.
Finally handed towel, dried off my hair.
Tousled, squeaky clean, with glitters.

I then sat down to have my supper
Like an outcast, was left to eat alone.
No one had waited for this lousy straggler,
Wearing company, they did not, condone.

But yes, I too, had learned a good lesson
Traveling visitors, not easily, out done.
Check out any company, new cow's keep,
For wearing cow lice, for sure, not any fun.

Photos by V. June Collins

Velma and Rue Freeman, Abalonian 1973

Jerry Collins, Ted Laufer, Velma and Props Freeman hauling in gear after successful catch.

*Velma and Rue were special friends for the enduring part of our lives, reaching back into the 1930's. We together hunted, camped, fished, and bottle hunted. Also rock-hounded, and hauled ever so many loads of rock home, on our backs, in packsacks, to wash clean, cut, polish, display and show at the Siskiyou Golden Fair, for a number of award winning years. Time, we were told, waits for no one. Gradually, and sadly one by one, they have been taken from us. I wrote Velma a poem for her eightieth birthday 9-12-1993, and eighty fifth 9-12-98. Yet, too soon, received word, she was leaving us. 8-18-99. Again, I write her, to salve my sorrow. Though we are nearing, standing alone, we continue to be blessed by having their daughter Karen, (Babes) and her husband Ted Laufer, of San Francisco, plus two of Velma and Rue's grandsons, Floyd Freeman and wife Kay of Redding, California, and Paul, Feeeman and his wife Jennie of Yreka still circling our wagons. Thanks!*

## *Written For Twenty Fifth Anniversary*

## TO VELMA & RUE

11-10-55

By: V. June Collins

Here's to two rock hounds, with both hearts of gold,
And right now, this memento I shall attempt to unfold.
You walk down the road, with a hump in your back
With your nose to the ground, as if sniffing a track.

Watch you lug up the hill, another huge, sack of rocks,
And to come trooping home, just sagged in your socks.
But just look again, they have more than one dish
Yes, one is for Hunting, and another is for Fish.

As each season goes round, it's with them, we all go
Sampling of each, thru much wind, rain and snow.
Into memories niche, we have carved a large space
Here smiling, but weary, still with mud on our face.

But some of the happenings, bring light to our eyes;
Both wide grins, and a laugh, and even some sighs.
Thinking back thru the years, with smiles on our lips,
More queer things have happened, the puns and the wit.

I see Velma switching words, often, backwards around,
As we rollic merrily, in mirth, from its rebounding sound.
I'm happy, and so glad, my life being ever so full, and
For Jerry my helper, with all of his melarky and bull.

Rue that old devil, whose teasings an art,
And Spot his big dog, thinks it's real smart,
For when he get one, with a wham! on the rear,
He still gallops around, as if it weren't clear.

He just sits, and he looks, and waggles his tail
Rue sure is his hero, with love that won't fail.
But when I hear them talking, in quiet alone,
I think this attachment, is mutually shown.

For it's only some times, in the dead of the night, I hear,
"You Black & White so 'n so! As Spot heaves out of sight.
Now don't forget Deek, dog, with his all welcoming grin,
Whose so happy, to see you, when e'er you come in.

So here's to 25 more, real happy, long years
For another wondrous occasion, and sight.
May your many more, between, silver and gold,
Also be, so "Shiney and Bright."
(or just maybe, Shite & Briney)

# BARN SOUR

*(When horses become ol' Coots)*

By V. June Collins

Might sound to you like a smelly place
But your first look, not always facts
Yes, most people that like horses
Don't even resent the smell of tracks.

Horse smells seem to grow with you
Wet saddle blankets prove a point.
It takes scads of them on each horse
To smooth out gaits and style anoint.

If separated for a time from ol' Coots,
That open barn door smells quite good.
That is, if you really do like horses
Like most folks working horses, should.

Today, ol' Coot pushed my buttons
Like a few do, this time of year.
Winter was an especially long one.
Have not yet got 'em into gear.

To ride him away from his old barn
That has sheltered him so well,
Again has been one up hill battle.
Shall take a bit of time to tell.

My legs, they're sure getting tired
Trying to keep his course straight.
Leggin' right and left, I'm determined
Will get him on a past that gate.

His head most like it's on a spring
And is anchored hard to yonder barn.
His mind is one-wayed, all made up.
This good horse has lost his charm.

He, like others, just got renamed
While name seems to fit and suit.
Today, he got my favorite old one,
That danged old stubborn "Coot".

I've finally got him to the hills,
Though near pooped and feel a mess.
He's still dreamin' of the barn
Will look good to me too, I confess.

Today, he's a barn sour old bastard.
Why, my thoughts could almost kill.
'Cause I know, when we get start back
He'll turn eager, like its all down hill.

Will then be as hard to hold him back
As it was pushing him, to ride away.
Sometimes it almost breaks my spirit.
But today, ol' COOT, Is not the day!

I've had a bit of practice, trial and error.
Some's bound to stick, when live this long.
Though on some it takes a lot more time.
Seldom is law of averages, all found wrong.

His barn sure will end up a place of work.
For him, might turn into a joy to leave.
"Ol' Coot," don't know the practices planned...
For weaning from barn, I have up sleeve.

**Notation and research, by :V. June Collins & Dan Weimar.**

   Still in our year 2003, scars can be plainly seen on the hillside above. Here at the mouth of Shasta River where the Shasta River empties into the Klamath River on old Highway 99, East of Yreka, California. During my studying of Siskiyou County Geology in 1950's with Walter Polluck, it was brought to our attention that when this huge slide occurred, the Klamath River was blocked for 4 days, where its restless waiting pressures, bent on release, accumulated. Until, like a desperate stampeding tidal wave, bent on meeting the ocean, it descended down stream with violent wrath, undoubtedly, in a mighty wall of water, *and I neglected to record the date- (V. J.C.)*

   On a field trip in 2002, with Dan Weimer as one of the historians, Dan told us of his research into some early 1861 records. These records had caused him to make note, as he read the man's recorded statement, of seeing a giant, twenty foot wall of water decend down the Klamath River, below Happy Camp, California. At that time, the cause was ***unknown.***

   Our combined research, leads us to believe our notations coincide, as the same year the big slide occurred. The slide possibly having been triggered by an earthquake.

**Photos: By V. June Collins**

# COWBOY POETRY ALONG THE TRAIL
Has been my pleasure.

Photo's By V. June Collins

## AND BARN SOUR VERSE
Of the stay at home variety.

COLD HATS, EVEN AFTER SO MANY GREAT RIDES,
will give you a wink, now and then.

INDEX        (*Italic Print* =Photo)

### A
| | |
|---|---|
| About Author *V, June Blevins Collins* | iv |
| After Christmas *and photo* | 242 |
| Among My Pages Are: | 257 |
| Appreciation and Acknowledgement | i |

### B
| | |
|---|---|
| Baling Twine *Photo* | 216 |
| Baling Wire | 215 |
| Barn Sour (ol' Coots) | 250 |
| *Beating The Heat..........1967* | 95 |
| Bebe *the burro and Tappy, Photo* | 170 |
| Blizzard Bier | 105 |
| *Blue* | 59 |
| *Boots without bronks, shootin' bull* | 107 |
| Brand Registration, 1915-- I. M. Blevins | 12 |
| Branding (explanation) | 16 |
| Branding Time | 17 |
| Brands, I. M. Blevins 1890 brand book | 13 |
| *Brewer Family,-Dean, Candy, and V. June* | 82 |
| Bronze Dansay (Dancer) | 67 |
| Buckskin Acres *(Splash, and Remodel)* | 123 |
| *Buckskin and Duns Dozing* | 122 |

### C
| | |
|---|---|
| Call Of The Wind *and drawings* | 85 |
| *Camp Creek Boat Ramp, Wiley Cow Used* | 181 |
| Candy and Natural Sweet | 76 |
| *Candy, Artise and Cappie* | 75 |
| *Chief Joseph Trail Rides* | 158 |
| Chow Time.................1970 | 111 |
| *Coe with Mike when a foal* | 30 |
| Cow's Reputation | 246 |
| Cowboy In Cabbage Patch 1972,*Keith* Severns | 126 |
| *Cowboy Poetry, Hats Awake and Asleep* | 253 |
| *Cowboy Sculpture, By Starritt* | 188 |
| Cowboy | 187 |
| Cultivating He Goes | 83 |
| Currie 1990 | 182 |

### D
| | |
|---|---|
| Damper Smart | 9 |
| Dedication *V. June and Jerry Collins* | ii |
| Distant Whispers *and painting* | 53 |
| Doc *(DoctorAlbert Newton)* | 73-74 |
| *Domino and V.June* | 195 |
| Domino | 196 |
| Don's Runway Golf Cart | 185 |
| Dreams | 222 |

### E
| | |
|---|---|
| Early And Late | 109 |
| Early Start | 1 |
| *Evelyn, Sprout and June* | 24 |

### F
| | |
|---|---|
| Fence Fixin' and *Photo* | 41 |

| | |
|---|---|
| *Fence with wires dropped for winter* | 40 |
| Fences | 37 |
| Flight Of The Runaway Truck Ramp | 225 |
| *Forks of Salmon Bridge after 1964 Flood* | 90 |
| Friend Of Friends.......1975 | 169 |
| *Friendships Endure 1928 - 2003 --* | 179 |

**H**

| | |
|---|---|
| Happy Buck-Appy..........1973 | 128 |
| Harrington Lake Or Bust | 142 |
| Hayrack Chores | 15 |
| Hayrack Chores (dedication) | 14 |
| Homeward Bound (*Blue*) | 59-60 |
| *Horse Tracks On Mt Shasta* | 113 |
| Hungry Waters........1965 | 87 |

**I**

| | |
|---|---|
| Introduction | iii |
| Jacket Retreat +*Photo* | 91 |
| *Jesse on Bogie* | 79 |
| Jim | 27 |
| *June. Keith Severns Mexico Olymp1968* | 168 |

**K**

| | |
|---|---|
| *Kentucky Rides* | 195 |
| *Klamath River Flood Scars* | 252 |

**L**

| | |
|---|---|
| Legend of Siskiyou | 116 |
| Life's Poem Pages | Zb-Zc |
| *Locust Tree Post Raymond Place* | 58 |
| Long Shirt-tail *and photo* | 21 |

**M**

| | |
|---|---|
| Mike (The Clydesdale) | 31 |
| Mileage Check | 234 |
| *Monte and family* | 6 |
| Monte | 7 |
| My After Thoughts (1993) | 99 |

**N**

| | |
|---|---|
| *Nadine Rogers, Wilhelmina Warick* | 260 |
| New Cows Reputation | 247 |
| Night Before Christmas | 239 |
| *Noon Hour Reprieve Painting* | 49 |
| Noon Hour Reprieve | 50 |

**O**

| | |
|---|---|
| Ochoco Rendezvous ( East of Prineville) | 176 |
| Off Balance (*old mowing machine blades*) | 209 |
| Ol' Gin Bob | 202 |
| *Old Malloy Fence* | 38 |
| Old Pinch Bottom | 208 |
| On The Smoky "C"......1969 | 107 |
| Other Boot Reasons | 238 |

**P**

| | |
|---|---|
| Pa and Charlie | 11 |
| Packers, Brogans And Lacers | 235 |
| Parts And Pieces | 230 |
| Passion *painting* | 66 |

| | |
|---|---|
| *Pink photo* | 137 |
| Pinks Call..............1974 | 172 |
| Pinks Day | 134 |
| Poetry's Assumed Names | 101 |
| *Pole Gate* | 37 |
| Politition's Mistake | 218 |
| Pollen Spring Pollen | 112 |

**R**

| | |
|---|---|
| Ramrod Brewer.........1966 | 80 |
| Rock and Walk | 190 |
| *Runaway Truck Ramps* | 224 |

**S**

| | |
|---|---|
| *Salmon River* | 210 |
| *Scars along The Klamath* | 253 |
| Second Childhood | 220 |
| Severns' Dog, Ruff | 165 |
| *Sheep Rock Photos* | 71 |
| Sheep Rock | 72 |
| *Six Hard Spots Six Stones* | 115 |
| Snow Comes Again In April...1967 | 92 |
| *Sonny Currie on Cooley, with Hought* | 180 |
| Sound Barrier | 207 |
| *Split Rail Corral* | 44 |
| Springs Restless Sunshine | 93 |
| Sprout | 25 |
| *Stan Cooley* | 212 |
| Stan's Stone Boatin' Steer | 212 |
| Such Is My Life | A to Z+ Za-Zb |
| Sulphur (*The Buckskin Filly*) | 102 |
| Sunset On Sheep Rock | 72 |

**T**

| | |
|---|---|
| Tailholt, *Mailboxes* | 244 |
| Tango, and *Tango photo* | 45 |
| *To Elko For Another Year* | 233 |
| Tracks | 63 |
| *Tracks photo* | 62 |
| Trail Class.............1975 | 133 |

**V**

| | |
|---|---|
| *V. June and Three Wheeler* | 192 |
| Velma & Rue Freeman *and Photo* | 248 |
| Virginia Josephine | 33 |

**W**

| | |
|---|---|
| Way It Is | 201 |
| We Have Legends | 114 |
| What Age- (Watt-Age) | 243 |
| Wheels To Deal | 191 |
| Wicked Wire Of The West | 55 |
| Wills, Wiles and Wont's | 228 |
| Wistful Wildernes *and Painting* | 146 |
| Wont's Of Youth | 200 |

**Y**

| | |
|---|---|
| Yellowstone Appy's | 159 |
| Yellowstone Ride | 157-158 |

# THOSE AMONG MY PAGES

ARNOLD RAY -W
BACA ALICIA -W
BACA CONCHA -W
BATSON ERMINE "BATTIE -U-V-W
BLEVINS AWILDA JOSEPHINE O'KELLEY -A-B-P-2-3-4-6-7-8-9-10-33-53-90-96-99-246
BLEVINS CORA J."COE" MILLER -A-B-M-P-Q-6-11-17-18-30-176
BLEVINS EVELYN IRENE -A-B-P-1-6-24-27
BLEVINS ISSAC MADISON -M-P-11-12-14-17-27-31-42-43-176
BLEVINS LEE EDWARD -A-B-M-P-Q-R-S-1-3-4-6-7-8-9-33
BLEVINS PENELTON -14
BLEVINS PENELTON -14
BOTTOMILLER Mrs. -5
BOYNTON MELVINA - 89
BRAZIL JACK -W
BRAZIL ROSALEE -W
BREWER "CAPPIE" JESS -75-82
BREWER ARTISE -75-82
BREWER CANDICE "CANDY -75-76-77-78-82
BROWN LEO -90
BROWN ROSE - i -90
BRYAN AL "SARG " -74
CORDOZA TOMMY -U
CAUBLE DON -185-186
CLEMENTS VIRGINIA"GIGE" LEE BLEVINS -33
CLINE SOULE - 244
COLLINS CAROLYN PUGH - E-Z-95-96-108-142-143-144-149-153
COLLINS GREGORY - 90-95-108-142-143-144-145-150
COLLINS LAEL - E-V-Z-Za-95-95-105-141-143-144-147-149-185
COLLINS MICHAEL"MIKE" LEE -E-U-Za-105
COLLINS TRACY - 98
COLLINS JERRY - i-E-I-U-X-83-84-95-102-105-107-115-142-147-154-155-157-164-239-242
COOLEY BETTY - i 212
COOLEY STAN -212-213-214
CORDOZA ANNA -U
COZZOLIO JAN - Z
CURRIE "SMOKE" - 107
CURRIE CODY -141-143-144-150
CURRIE SONNY - 180-181-182-184
DEIHM BILL - i
DENTON HAZEL SMITH - 176-177-179
DENTON HAZEL SMITH - 178-179
DONNELLEY ALEX - 9
FREEMAN RUE - 21-248-249

GARNER GORDON -179
GARNER VERDON -179
GESSNER DOC -5
GRUBB VALOURA WORK JOHNSON -179
KEETON ELVA MAE -179
KEETON OMA -179
KEN KLINE -185-186
LANIUS HESTER -179
LEMOS AGNES -51-95-96-127
LEMOS ERNIE -57-95-96 E
LEMOS STELL -45
MABEL RUTH (OKELLEY) ZEVELY -33
MARLOW GARY - i
MARSKE "AL" -W
MARTIN PAT LEIGH -223
McCOMBS ARRON -107
McCOMBS JIM -107
McCURDY DICK -97
MEAMBER BERNICE SOULE -244
MILLER SAMUEL W. -14
MILLER DR. PAUL - 174
MOTT DEAN -82
NENTL"SALLY" HINDERMAN -179
NEWTON DR ALBERT -73-74
OKELLEY LYDIA C. ELLIOTT -6
PAGE CHARLIE -54
ROBERTSON THELMA SMITH -179
ROGERS NADINE -i-260
ROSE DAVID LEE - i
SEVERNS JUNE -95-96-107 108-134-142-143-148-150-151-159-168-180-233
SEVERNS KEITH -95-96-107-108-126-134-142-143-147 to 149-152-157-165 to 169 -180
SHERIFF RICHARDSON -48
SLEEP DAVID -67
SMITH ROY -190
SMITH SYLVIA -178-179
STARRETT MINERVA "MIN" -189
STARRETT RALPH -188-189
VELMA FREEMAN -248-249
WARICK WILHELMINA -i-260
WEIMER DAN -252
WINDER "HAP" -105

*I have found that others, as well as myself, when browsing through pages of any new book, of interest, turn first, to the back of the book. So like many others, you too, have now arrived at a beginning. Where, "Two Staunch Supporters," are waiting, and will greet you on your reading journey, be it, from its beginning or its end. -- Enjoy!*

 NADINE & WILHELMINA

We've covered nicks and crannies,
Inside the pages of this book.
When, I see your two smiling faces,
Again, I turn, and take another look.
So special is this warmth of friendship
It surges through me and my soul.
I'm so blessed by God, to have savored
Your two friendships, that make a whole.
We met at Siskiyou Writer's Club.
Seems 1993, to be, about the year.
We're allowed, to savor of this friendship
As feel of a warmth, and closeness, adhere.
Yes, among the sharing, of my life's stories,
You became part of the pages of this book.
And for your pictures, in review,
I Thank you!
" As I take another smiling, look!"

V. J. C.